EPHESIANS

NCCS | *New Covenant Commentary Series*

The New Covenant Commentary Series (NCCS) is designed for ministers and students who require a commentary that interacts with the text and context of each New Testament book and pays specific attention to the impact of the text upon the faith and praxis of contemporary faith communities.

The NCCS has a number of distinguishing features. First, the contributors come from a diverse array of backgrounds in regards to their Christian denominations and countries of origin. Unlike many commentary series that tout themselves as international the NCCS can truly boast of a genuinely international cast of contributors with authors drawn from every continent of the world (except Antarctica) including countries such as the United States, Australia, the United Kingdom, Kenya, India, Singapore, and Korea. We intend the NCCS to engage in the task of biblical interpretation and theological reflection from the perspective of the global church. Second, the volumes in this series are not verse-by-verse commentaries, but they focus on larger units of text in order to explicate and interpret the story in the text as opposed to some often atomistic approaches. Third, a further aim of these volumes is to provide an occasion for authors to reflect on how the New Testament impacts the life, faith, ministry, and witness of the New Covenant Community today. This occurs periodically under the heading of "Fusing the Horizons." Here authors provide windows into community formation (how the text shapes the mission and character of the believing community) and ministerial formation (how the text shapes the ministry of Christian leaders).

It is our hope that these volumes will represent serious engagements with the New Testament writings, done in the context of faith, in service of the church, and for the glorification of God.

Series Editors:
Michael F. Bird (Bible College of
   Queensland, Australia)
Craig Keener (Palmer Seminary,
   Philadelphia, USA)

Titles in this series:
Romans Craig Keener
Colossians and Philemon Michael F. Bird

Forthcoming titles (in order of projected publication):

Revelation Gordon Fee
James Pablo Jimenez
1–3 John Sam Ngewa
John Jey Kanagaraj
Pastoral Epistles Aída Besançon-Spencer
Mark Kim Huat Tan
Acts Youngmo Cho & Hyung Dae Park
Luke Jeannine Brown

2 Peter and Jude Andrew Mbuvi
Matthew Joel Willits
1 Peter Eric Greaux
1–2 Thessalonians David E. Garland
Philippians Linda Belleville
Hebrews Tom Thatcher
Galatians Brian Vickers
2 Corinthians David deSilva

EPHESIANS

A New Covenant Commentary

Lynn H. Cohick

CASCADE *Books* · Eugene, Oregon

EPHESIANS
A New Covenant Commentary

New Covenant Commentary Series 10

Cascade Books
An Imprint of Wipf and Stock Publishers
199 W. 8th Ave., Suite 3
Eugene, OR 97401

www.wipfandstock.com

ISBN 13: 978-1-60608-141-9

Cataloguing-in-Publication data:

Cohick, Lynn H.

    Ephesians : a new covenant commentary / Lynn H. Cohick.

    xiv + 176 p. ; 23 cm. Includes bibliographical references and indexes.

    New Covenant Commentary Series 10

    ISBN 13: 978-1-60608-141-9

    1. Bible. N.T. Ephesians—Commentaries. I. Title. II. Series.

BS2695.3 C55 2010

Manufactured in the U.S.A.

for
James Allen Cohick Jr.

Contents

Preface

Ambrosiaster[1] does well in trying to capture the volume and brilliance of the vision of the Triune God expounded in the six chapters of Ephesians. Pointing to the phrase "length and breadth and depth and height" (3:18), he asks his readers to think of a sphere, whose length is the same as its breadth, and whose depth is the same as its height. He rejoices that the same is true of God, who is boundlessly infinite. Ambrosiaster observes that we cannot thank God enough who, being infinite and infinitely great, yet made possible humanity's redemption through Christ. Julian of Norwich had a vision of a different sort of sphere, specifically a hazelnut, which seemed so small and insignificant that it might disintegrate into nothingness. This nut symbolized the universe in relationship to God, and she marveled that God would care for something so relatively inconsequential. But she understood that it was God's vast love which sustained it. In meditating on the great love of God shown in his redemption of humanity from sin, she cried that "all shall be well, and all shall be well, and all manner of thing shall be well."[2]

The Letter to the Ephesians invites its readers to sing with Julian that all shall be well. In this epistle, sin has been overcome by Christ's death on the cross. Saved by God's grace through faith, Christians are seated with Christ in the heavens. They enjoy full fellowship through Christ's work in making the two (Jew and Gentile) into one holy people, a temple of the Lord, the Body of Christ. Sealed with the Holy Spirit, they are empowered for holy living.

It has been my joy to wade into this epistle, with its exuberant, extravagant language that, like a stained glass window lit up by the sun's rays, casts a radiant picture of God and his church. I offer my deepest thanks to Craig Keener and Michael Bird for their invitation to participate in the New Covenant Commentary Series. Their shrewd comments helped me think more clearly and strengthened my arguments. My sin-

1. Ambrosiaster, *Epistle to the Ephesians* 3.18.2, in CSEL 81.3:93.
2. Julian of Norwich, *Revelations of Divine Love*.

cere appreciation goes to the editorial team at Wipf and Stock, especially Chris Spinks, who made the publishing process smooth and efficient. I am indebted to Wheaton College and my dean, Jill Baumgaertner, and associate dean, Jeffrey Greenman, for providing release time to pursue this delightful project. I am deeply grateful to my colleague Michael Graves for our fruitful dialogues on the Greek text of Ephesians. My teaching assistant, Adam Cieszkiewicz, exceeded the call of duty in his diligent research, proofreading, and insightful suggestions for content in the Fusing the Horizons sections. I am truly thankful for the loving support of my children, Sarah and C. J. I dedicate this book to my husband, Jim, who has never failed to love me "just as Christ loved the church and gave himself for her" (Eph 5:25).

Abbreviations

AB	Anchor Bible
ANTC	Abingdon New Testament Commentaries
CSEL	Corpus scriptorum ecclesiasticorum latinorum
ICC	International Critical Commentary
JBL	*Journal of Biblical Literature*
JSNTSup	Journal for the Study of the New Testament, Supplement Series
NovTSup	Supplements to Novum Testamentum
PG	Patrologia graece, edited by J.-P. Migne, 162 vols. (Paris, 1857–86)
PL	Patrologia latina, edited by J.-P. Migne, 217 vols. (Paris, 1844–64)
TynBul	*Tyndale Bulletin*
SNTSMS	Society for New Testament Studies Monograph Series
SP	Sacra pagina
WBC	Word Biblical Commentary
WUNT	Wissenschaftliche Untersuchungen zum Neuen Testament

ANCIENT SOURCES

Aristotle
Pol.   *Politica* (*Politics*)

Augustine
Ep.   *Epistulae* (*Letters*)

Cicero
Att.   *Epistulae ad Atticum* (*Letters to Atticus*)
Fam.   *Epistulae ad familiares* (*Letters to Friends*)
Quint. fratr.   *Epistulae ad Quintum fratrem* (*Letters to Quintus*)

1 Clem.   *1 Clement*

Abbreviations

Clement of Alexandria
Strom.   *Stromata* (*Miscellanies*)

Dio Chrysostom
2 Serv. lib.   *De servitude et libertate ii* (*Or. 15*)
                      (*On Slavery and Freedom 2*)

Diogenes Laertius
Lives   *Lives of Eminent Philosophers*

Epictetus
Diatr.   *Diatribai* (*Discourses*)

Eusebius
Hist. eccl.   *Historia ecclesiastica* (*Ecclesiastical History*)

Herodotus
Hist.   *Historiae* (*Histories*)

Jerome
Comm. Eph.   *Commentariorum in epistulam ad Ephesios libri III*
                      (*Commentary on St. Paul's Epistle to the Ephesians*)

John Chrysostom
Sac.   *De sacerdotio* (*On the Priesthood*)
Hom. Eph.   *Homiliae in epistulam ad Ephesios* (*Homilies on
                      Ephesians*)

Josephus
Ant.   *Jewish Antiquities*
J.W.   *Jewish War*

Martin Luther
Papacy   *On the Papacy in Rome, against the Illustrious
                      Romanists in Leipzig* (1520)

Origen
Cels.   *Contra Celsum* (*Against Celsus*)
Princ.   *De principiis* (*Peri Archōn*) (*On First Principles*)

Pliny the Younger
Ep. Epistulae (*Letters*)

Plutarch
Am. prol. De amore prolis (*On Affection for Offspring*)

Polybius
Hist. Historia (*Histories*)

Quintilian
Inst. Institutio oratoria (*The Institutes*)

Seneca
Ben. De beneficiis (*On Benefits*)
Ep. Epistulae morales (*Moral Essays*)
Ira De ira (*On Anger*)

Tertullian
Marc. Adversus Marcionem (*Against Marcion*)

Thomas Aquinas
Comm. Eph. Super Epistolam B. Pauli ad Ephesios lectura
(*Commentary on Saint Paul's Epistle to the Ephesians*)

Introduction

Overview of Paul's Letter to the Ephesians

Perhaps no letter in the Pauline corpus takes the reader to such mountain heights of adoration and to such level fields of practicality as the six short chapters of Ephesians do. One might call it a feast for the Christian imagination, for it lays out the gospel with great depth and intellectual texture. Paul[1] reflects on the magnificence, even lavishness, of God's redemptive work established in Christ and continued in the Spirit. Chrysostom remarks how Paul grasped the eternal plan of God, connecting Paul's thought with Christ's own words in Matt 25:34 to the faithful that he will welcome them into the kingdom prepared for them from the foundation of the world.[2] Paul explores the intricacies of what this kingdom looks like for the church now and in the future, as he fills out the picture of the Triune God who from the beginning has orchestrated this grand movement of salvation. Jerome, likely following Origen, acknowledged the complexity of Paul's thought in describing God's free gift of salvation. Recall, Jerome remarks, that Ephesus in Paul's day had at its center the great temple of Artemis/Diana and the widely practiced magical arts commanding allegiance and attention of all its dwellers and visitors. Paul's letter taught deep theological realities about the powers and principalities against which believers do battle, for the Ephesians were in the thick of the fight.[3] Martin Luther, in his theological disagreement with the Roman Catholic Church, argued that Ephesians (4:5) expressed Paul's vision of the church as the one true body of believers united by one heart even though separated physically by thousands of miles.[4] Luther's

1. Pauline authorship of Ephesians is debated, and a detailed discussion of the matter is found later in this chapter.

2. John Chrysostom *Hom. Eph.* 1.

3. Jerome *Comm. Eph.*, preface, bk. 1.

4. Martin Luther, *Papacy* (1520).

1

comments reflect the general Christian debate about the nature of the church, which has continued through the centuries and relies in large part on Paul's understanding of the church expressed in Ephesians. As these three examples show, Ephesians covers key foundational aspects of the gospel, including Christology, pneumatology, soteriology, eschatology, and ecclesiology. To these we might add the modern questions of authorship and the social roles described in chapter 5. In Ephesians we find much to reflect upon as God's plan of redemption, and our own part in the story, is laid before us. The first chapter of Ephesians presents with rhetorical flourish and fanfare the praise rightly due to the one true God, Father, Son, and Spirit. The stage lights are first focused on God the Father, who chose to redeem the world for his good purposes, including creating a people unto himself in Christ. In chapter 2 the spotlight grows to include more fully the role of Christ Jesus in the plan of salvation, and with chapter 3 the stage is flooded with light, revealing the activities of the Holy Spirit in accomplishing the goals of salvation within the church. The final three chapters direct attention to the church, this new creation based on the work of Christ and empowered by the Spirit for God's glory. Why start with the Trinity? Whatever Paul's reason, it has the effect of re-inforcing the amazingly simple, but profound truth that God is the center of the universe. Not my salvation, not my social justice concerns, not my doctrines on ecclesiology or eschatology; God is the center, the beginning and the end. The tremendous idea—Paul trips over his words to make sense of it—is that the majestic God has determined in our time to make known his salvation plan in Christ. Through the Spirit, he set in motion the salvation plan for a new creation and the full realization of the king-dom of God. If we start with Ephesians in our quest to understand the gospel as Paul outlines it (instead of starting with Romans, for example, although the two letters share quite a bit in common), we might register aspects of Paul's message that have been muffled or ignored. For example, Ephesians stresses God's grace in the forgiveness of sins for the purpose of building a new community, a holy temple dedicated to God's glory. God acted in Christ through the Spirit to make a new creation, which includes personal forgiveness of sins *so that* a people (Jew and Gentile, slave and free, male and female) might be made into a new household of God for his glory.

Though difficult to reduce such a complex argument as we find in Ephesians into a single sentence, a possible statement might be that through Christ, God the Father has redeemed humanity from sin and has created a new people empowered by the Spirit. The following outline highlights Paul's major thought units:

I. Introduction
>   A. 1:1–2: Paul's Greetings

II. Redemption in Christ makes the Two One
>   A. 1:3–14: God's Work of Salvation
>   B. 1:15–23: Christ's Rule over All Things
>   C. 2:1–10: Saved by Grace Alone
>   D. 2:11–22: Christ Our Peace Builds His Church

III. Mystery of Salvation Seen in Paul's Imprisonment
>   A. 3:1–13: God's Salvation Plan Revealed
>   B. 3:14–21: Paul's Prayer for Believers' Wisdom and Fullness

IV. Exhortation to Walk Worthy of Our Calling
>   A. 4:1–16: One Spirit, One Lord, One God and Father, One Body
>   B. 4:17–24: Put on the New Person
>   C. 4:25–32: Speak Truth in Love
>   D. 5:1–14: Imitate God, Walk in Love
>   E. 5:15–21: Be Filled with the Spirit
>   F. 5:22—6:9: Spirit-Filled Relationships in Christ
>   G. 6:10–20: Put on the Armor of God

V. Closing Remarks
>   A. 6:21–24: Paul's Final Words of Grace and Peace

MODERN INTERPRETIVE QUESTIONS

Since the 1960s, a most heated discussion has enveloped the interpretation of Paul. Two camps emerged, known, with a singular lack of creativity, as the old perspective and the new perspective. The "old" way of reading Paul is to stress his emphasis on forgiveness of sins and justification of the individual sinner through Christ's work on the cross and his resurrection. The new perspective challenges that Paul was quite interested in the relationship between Jews and Gentiles and how the work of Christ affects each community as well as the newly forming church. In Ephesians, we have both of these convictions represented as two sides of the same coin. The redemptive work of Christ takes material shape in creating a new people of God made up of Jews and Gentiles. The new community is not a serendipitous result of Christ's resurrection; rather it is the tangible, everyday proof of God's surpassing power to make all things new. The empty tomb evidences Christ's resurrection, and his appearance to his disciples and apostles (including Paul, 1 Cor 9:1–2; 15:8) was a testimony many clung to even in the face of martyrdom. But the ramifications of the resurrection are not limited to the salvation of the human soul, or even to restoring the kingdom to Israel as the disciples wondered aloud to Jesus (Acts 1:6). God's plans are much bigger. They include the whole creation, and the evidence of Jew and Gentile together as equal participants in community is the daily confirmation Paul points to that God is indeed at work in Christ. The Letter to the Ephesians is a six-chapter exposition on the mystery of God's wisdom revealed in this salvation plan.

Ironically, those who reject Pauline authorship of the letter (see a full discussion below) often point to the focused attention the church receives in Ephesians for support of their contentions. But the emphasis on church is a natural and essential aspect of Christ's work on the cross, and so the extensive discussion in Ephesians about the church should not give rise to suspicions that the letter is deutero-Pauline, that is, attributed to Paul but not written under Paul's direct influence. Indeed the church is a necessary part of God's redemptive plan, which is to make all creation new. The church, as the body of Christ (who is its head), is an instrument through which God works to restore his creation, until the final event when God will establish the new heavens and new earth, when Christ hands over the kingdom to the Father (1 Cor 15:28). The church as the body of Christ represents (imperfectly) Christ to the world, and as such it is not a pleasant, though secondary, consequence of God's work of redemption. Instead the church signals, by the empowering Spirit, the gospel to the unbelieving and seeking world. Said another way, the church is best understood, not as a collection of saved individuals or a group pledging particular doctrines (Catholic, Orthodox, Protestant), but as a living organism. By walking in the good works prepared for it by God (Eph 2:10), the church led by Christ, the head, witnesses to God's power and love. Ephesians pushes us toward a healthy vision of the church and away from a purely individualistic understanding of salvation.

AUTHORSHIP OF EPHESIANS

Pauline authorship of Ephesians is contested, with several reasons put forward to suggest Paul did not write the epistle. For some, the language, its terms and grammar, sound too different from the undisputed letters (Romans, Galatians, 1 and 2 Corinthians, Philippians, 1 Thessalonians, Philemon) to be written by the same hand. For others, the theology, especially ecclesiology and soteriology, are sufficiently distinct to warrant pause in proclaiming Pauline authorship. Again, the apparent acceptance of Greco-Roman social status quo—the hierarchy of father, wife, children, slaves—speaks against this letter being written by the same author who penned 1 Corinthians. These concerns should not be dismissed lightly; however, they are capable of interpretation in a way that holds to Pauline authorship. Moreover, postulating a deutero-Pauline status for Ephesians does not solve all problems; indeed, it can create new ones, such as demonstrating the relative acceptance of pseudonymous[5] authorship and pseudepigraphic[6] work in the ancient world, their acceptance within the early church, and the reason for detailed personal information in Ephesians. In the end, I suggest the balance of the evidence weighs on the side of Pauline authorship, but I invite the readers to examine the evidence below to satisfy themselves on the matter.

Ancient Letter-Writing Practices

The letter itself claims to be from Paul, who states his name and then describes himself as an apostle of Christ Jesus (1:1) and later as a prisoner of Christ Jesus (3:1, see also 4:1, 6:20). Most of the undisputed letters begin with Paul declaring himself an apostle of Christ Jesus, although the formula is not rigidly followed, for in 1 Cor 1:1 he declares he was called as an apostle, while to the Romans he announces himself a slave of Christ Jesus who was called to be an apostle. The opening description of Paul in Ephesians, then, does not present any immediate hint of irregularity

---

5. This term for our purposes does not include *nom de plume* such as Samuel Clemens' pen name Mark Twain.

6. Pseudepigraphy is a label of a work whose author uses another, usually better known name, while pseudepigrapha refers to a particular set of extra-canonical or post-canonical works. The term pseudonymity identifies the author as using another name, which may take the form of a *nom de plume* or a borrowed name from a well-known author.

concerning authorship. Nor does the statement that Paul was a prisoner suggest pseudonymity. Paul notes in 2 Cor 11:23 that he has been imprisoned numerous times. He speaks of himself as a prisoner in Phlm 1, 9, and as being in chains in Col 4:3, 18. Acts 16:23–26 indicates that Paul was put in stocks, chained in an inner part of the prison in Philippi. The evidence raises at least two questions: Would someone writing in Paul's name have included his claims of imprisonment? And were these chains seen in a positive or negative light? Looking at the first question, did Paul's numerous imprisonments become a leitmotif of Paul's life such that any person writing decades after Paul would need to include reference to his chains? This answer is related to our second question, which might be answered in one of two ways, based on how we understand Paul's chains to be understood within the early church. In the larger society, being in chains was shameful; Paul likewise recognized that his chains could be understood in this way.[7] But he also celebrates them as a symbol of his apostleship and faithful witness to the gospel message's power to upset the religious and social status quo. One might argue that it would be rather presumptuous for an author to remake Paul's actual chains into a literary theme which served to encourage boldness and faithfulness in service to Christ. In the letters to Philemon and Colossae Paul reflects deeply on the reality of his chains; thus "for individuals to write in Paul's name and bind themselves, figuratively, with Paul's chains, a considerable audacity would be required."[8] Cassidy raises an important point often overlooked in authorship discussions, namely the fact that if Paul did not write the letter, then whoever did sought to speak not only with the apostle's voice, but with the authority of one who was in chains for Christ. Those claiming deutero-Pauline status usually explain that the disciple was writing in Paul's name to bring Paul's ethics and theology up to date for the new generation of believers. Surely that could be done without also assuming the moral authority of one who suffered so specifically and for such duration as Paul. The moral implications of claiming the voice of one who suffered greatly should give pause to the suggestions that one of Paul's own followers would strike such a pose.

Throughout both the disputed and undisputed Pauline letters, we have the author declaring that he is writing to his congregations, and to-

---

7. Rapske 1994: 283–312.

8. Cassidy 2001: 87.

day we imagine him sitting quietly at his desk, pen in hand etching strange Greek characters on papyrus scrolls. In the ancient world, however, most people did not write down their own letters but used the services of a scribe. In some cases it was a personal slave or employee, in others it was a hired service. In our particular situation, this means that Paul did not actually write *any* of his letters, if by that one means that he put pen to papyrus. Rather, Paul used the services of others, a scribe or amanuensis, to take down his letter. Thus when Paul declares to the Galatians or the Thessalonians that he is writing to them, he is describing his personal signature and closing remarks (Gal 6:11; 2 Thess 3:17). How much of the scribe's own personal style infused the letter? This is difficult to determine, but the range of scribal activity extends from taking dictation syllable by syllable, to composing a letter based on general instructions. In almost all cases, the author would review the letter draft before a final copy was made and sent. We also do not know if Paul used the same scribe several times. One scribe identifies himself as Tertius (Rom 16:22; see also 1 Pet 5:12), but we do not know if he wrote any of Paul's other letters. Romans was likely written from Corinth during Paul's third missionary journey, and we would have to postulate that Tertius was with Paul in other cities or over the course of his journeys to suppose that he wrote other letters, which is not an impossible scenario, but one for which we have no information. We should not forget that for several letters Paul is imprisoned (Philippians, Colossians, Philemon), which further complicates his options. We should pause for a moment to observe that Paul coauthors most of his letters; this fact has not usually penetrated discussions about authenticity. This is a rare, almost unique innovation, for we have no evidence that Cicero, Seneca, or Pliny the Younger, for example, ever coauthored a letter. It seems that Cicero's friend Atticus did write one letter with a group of people,[9] and Richards identified six coauthored letters out of the 645 private letters from the Oxyrhynchus corpus, but these are not at all similar to Paul's letters.[10] Only Romans, Galatians, Ephesians, and the Pastoral Epistles are authored by Paul alone (with the aid of a scribe). How involved were Titus, Timothy, and Sosthenes in the content and style of Paul's other letters? Was it merely courteous of Paul to note his coworkers, or did they have significant input with content and style? Anthony

---

9. Cicero *Att.* 11.5.1.

10. Richards 2004: 34.

Kenny explores this question with a stylometric analysis, focused not on key terms or unusual vocabulary, but on stylistic quirks and traits that an author expresses unconsciously. For example, those from Pittsburgh drink "pop" but in Philadelphia they drink "soda"; both use these synonyms unconsciously and thus reveal their backgrounds. Kenny observed the frequency of subordinate clauses and conjunctions (and, but), and discovered both great diversity and strong commonality between *all* of the Pauline letters.[11] Interestingly, letters closest to what is understood as the center of Paul's thought were those he wrote alone (with a secretary), namely Romans, Philippians, and 2 Timothy. Ephesians, heavily indebted to Colossians (coauthored by Timothy) is farther down the list, but still closer to the center than 1 Corinthians, the only letter coauthored with Sosthenes. This evidence suggests that Paul's coauthors might have played a larger role in the finished product than has been previously thought.

One final note about letters: in the ancient world, as today, they frequently substitute for the personal presence of the writer. Often Paul will declare that he longs to see his congregation, but must be satisfied with sending them a letter. The implication of this is that we expect that the author knows his audience well. For the most part this holds true for Paul's letters, with a few important exceptions. In the case of Romans, Paul is introducing himself to the Christian community in the imperial capital in hopes of soon visiting them. Similarly, Paul (with Timothy) writes to the Colossians with authority, although it is one of his coworkers, Epaphras, who founded the church. Yet in both cases, mutual friends are listed at the end of the letters. In fact, Romans has the longest list of personal friends, which might not be surprising if Paul is trying to form a relationship with the Roman church. What would be more natural than to cite common acquaintances? Ephesians lacks both a sense of intimacy with the congregation, as well as names of specific church members, which are unexpected, given that he spent over two years there according to Acts. However, Paul's communications to the Thessalonians has no personal references, even though Paul founded that church only a few months before writing his letters from Corinth (Acts 18:5; 1 Thess 3:6). Any explanation about Pauline authorship of Ephesians must take into account the relative lack of statements of personal knowledge about the addressees. Most explain this as indicating either that the letter was not written by Paul, or that the

11. Kenny 1986: 99–100.

letter was intended as an encyclical letter to be read by various churches in the vicinity of Ephesus.

External Evidence for Authorship

The latter possibility is reinforced by a particular textual variant. In some of the most reliable manuscripts, the words "in Ephesus" are not found in 1:1 as one would expect. Several questions immediately come to mind, such as whether Paul would write a letter that would be read to various churches. In Col 4:15–16, Paul requests that his letter to them be shared with the nearby city of Laodicea, and the letter he sent to the latter city (not extant) be read by the Colossians. Again, Galatians is also written to the churches in that province. From these examples we could at least conclude that Paul is not opposed to having several churches read each other's letters. Interestingly, an ancient writer, Marcion (declared a heretic for his views on the Jewish Bible/Old Testament and the person of Jesus) is reported by Tertullian to have identified Ephesians as Paul's letter to the Laodiceans, but it is unclear, however, whether Tertullian is speaking of the letter itself or the superscription (title page, if you will), and whether Marcion is supplying a missing text or changing an existing text.[12]

Further questions include whether the manuscripts without "in Ephesus" are accurate in their rendering, or whether there is some corruption whereby the relevant locale was omitted. The oldest sources, including P[46] (third century CE), Codex Sinaiticus and Codex Vaticanus (both fourth century CE), omit "in Ephesus" in the actual letter, but do include "to the Ephesians" in the superscription. These three manuscripts are of the Alexandrian text type, which suggests a local variant. The rest of the reliable manuscripts, from a variety of regions, including the early Coptic (Egyptian language) translation, incorporate the phrase "in Ephesus." This list includes the earliest editorial changes in both Sinaiticus and Vaticanus. Thus we have excellent external evidence for both readings. Finally, Origen, who lived both in Alexandria and in Caesarea Maritima, in his commentary on Ephesians seems not to have used a manuscript that had the words "in Ephesus." However, he makes it clear in the text that he believes Paul is writing to the Ephesians, as his opening line in the discussion of Eph 1:1 reads "In the case of Ephesians alone we find

12. Tertullian *Marc.* 5.11.12; 5.17.1.

the phrase 'to the saints who are.'"[13] He has a remarkable interpretation of the awkward Greek, namely that Paul is describing the Ephesians as those who once were not, but now are, through God. He takes his cue from Moses' encounter with God in the desert, when God reveals who he is by saying "I AM." In both cases, the verb for "to be" is used. Although we have only fragments of Origen's commentary on Ephesians preserved, Jerome clearly used it in composing his own commentary.[14] And he probably also used Origen's prologue as well, wherein Origen makes clear that the letter in question is addressed to the Ephesian church, suffering from an overwhelming attraction to magic and the goddess Diana (drawing on Acts 19:1–20).

If the manuscript evidence is inconclusive, the internal evidence might shift the balance. Usually textual critics prefer the more difficult reading and the shorter reading. If these rules are followed, the omission of the phrase in the original seems assured. In this case, the copyists, aware of the difficult reading, stayed true to the text in front of them, not smoothing out the reading. They would have no apparent reason for omitting the city's name. In fact, they might have assumed Paul was following the Hellenistic custom whereby a royal decree was often lacking a specific addressee because the declaration was to be read in numerous cities.[15]

However, a further critical rule suggests that if a variant reading is nonsensical or uncharacteristic of the author's work, the longer reading should be supported. In this case, the omission creates an odd reading in Greek and is uncharacteristic of Pauline letters. Normally we find Paul using "to those who are" followed by a place name in his introduction and greetings. Those manuscripts that omit the place name read awkwardly, "to the saints, to those who are, and believers in Christ Jesus." The problematic reading might be better explained as a copyist error than coming from the original text. Some suggest, however, that the omission indicates this letter was intended as an encyclical epistle to be read in several churches. It was up to Paul's envoy and letter carrier, Tychicus, to insert the city's name as he read it to the several churches in small cities in the vicinity of Ephesus. Although no copy of the letter has either a space in the manuscript for a city's name to be inserted or the preposition

---

13. Heine 2002: 80.
14. Ibid., 35.
15. Comfort 2008: 577–79.

"in" followed by a blank space, nonetheless, if Tychicus was instructed to insert the name of the city when he read it to the churches, there would be little need to leave a space in the actual text. We might pause for a moment and note that Paul gives Tychicus the responsibility to inform the listeners of his situation (this is true as well in Colossians). It seems that Paul instructed his envoys to communicate more than what was on the page, for example when he reveals in 2 Cor 7:6–16 that he expected Titus to reassure the Corinthians of Paul's concern for them. Again, the custom of reading the letter publicly to the church was apparently consistent throughout Pauline churches. Even a letter as personal as Philemon was read to the entire church, as indicated by the plural "you" at the beginning and end of the letter. Furthermore, the instructions that Tychicus give details of Paul's situation (in chains) suggests that the apparent lack of personal details in Ephesians itself might be counterbalanced by Tychicus and by Paul's personal knowledge of individual communities surrounding Ephesus. Paul's situation in prison might have prevented him from writing individual letters, but would not prevent Tychicus from passing along specific greetings and encouragements directed orally by Paul through him. An intriguing, but limited parallel could be drawn with contemporary papyrus invitations, many of which lack the name of the addressee. These one-line invitations to a birthday party, wedding, or other festivity depended upon the messenger to include the guest's name at the time the invitation was read to them.[16] In the end, it seems the evidence is weighed slightly in favor of the letter being addressed to the church in Ephesus, but given Paul's encouragement to the Colossians to share their letter with the Laodiceans, it is entirely possible that Tychicus, as he traveled from Ephesus to Colossae, read Paul's letter to the Ephesians to the satellite Christian communities orbiting around the central city of Ephesus.

Support for this possibility might come from 1 Corinthians, which was penned in Ephesus (1 Cor 16:8). In 1 Cor 16:19, Paul extends greetings from the churches in the province of Asia, which may signal that he sees the Ephesian Christian community not limited to the city limits, but extending to the towns beyond. "Paul here seems to imply . . . that the Christian community of Ephesus was the central Christian community of the province. . . . This suggests that the Ephesian Christian community was a missionary centre, and maintained contact with Christians in other

---

16. Kim 1975: 391–402.

parts of the province."[17] This follows the Roman assumption concerning the *polis* or city, which understood its influence to cover extensively the surrounding territory outside its walls. For example, even before Paul's time, most of Italy was seen as part of Rome, broadly speaking. Freeborn Italians had a form of Roman citizenship known as Latin rights citizenship. A similar attitude towards large urban centers outside of Rome continued in the imperial period.[18] This allows for the possibility that someone living even twenty miles (a day's journey) from the Ephesus city center might be considered (and consider themselves) an Ephesian. Clearly the limit did not extend to Colossae, one hundred miles from Ephesus, or Smyrna, thirty-five miles away.

Internal Evidence

Literary Character of Ephesians

The main internal concerns that surface in any conversation about Pauline authorship of Ephesians focus on the literary character, the theological emphases, and the historical setting implied in the letter. Turning to the first point, we can be more specific in highlighting the singular turns of phrase that some point to as indicative of a deutero-Pauline hand. For example, instead of the usual term "Satan" in Ephesians, Paul speaks of the "devil" (4:27, 6:11). Again, rather than his usual wording "the heavens," he speaks of "the heavenlies." These terms hardly indicate theological shifts, but because they are so insignificant they are thought to expose the author's automatic reflex. Since Paul would think automatically of the evil one as "Satan," the author of Ephesians, in using "devil," exposes himself as other than Paul. However, if we apply this logic to his other letters, we see that it is flawed. Paul can use synonyms for an idea or action, even within the same letter. He is not limited to a single term to express his ideas.[19] Again, the lengthy sentences and numerous participial phrases are pointed to as reasons to doubt that Paul composed the letter. For example, his opening thanksgiving runs from 1:3–14 (see also 1:15–23; 2:1–7; 3:2–13, 14–19; 4:1–6, 11–16; 6:14–20). But we find long sentences in other letters, especially when Paul writes doxologically (Rom 1:1–7,

17. Trebilco 2004: 71.
18. Lightstone 2005: 214–25.
19. Hoehner 2002: 24–26.

8:38-9, 11:33-39; 1 Cor 1:4-8; Phil 1:3-8; and 2 Thess 1:3-10) or about doctrine (Rom 3:21-26; 1 Cor 1:26-29), or concerning ethical matters (compare Eph 6:14-20; 1 Cor 12:8-11; and Phil 1:27—2:11). In the past, statistical analysis was used to support a deutero-Pauline position. But more recently this method has been called into question, due in no small part to the lack of material by Paul himself. Even though he has written many letters in the New Testament, the actual corpus is relatively small, failing to provide a statistically significant amount of words from which to draw conclusions. Even more, when Ephesians is compared, for example, with the uncontested Galatians, the results are surprising. The letters are about the same length, and each contain about the same number of terms occurring only in that epistle (41 terms out of 2,429 in Ephesians, 35 terms [or 31 if you subtract proper names] out of 2,220 in Galatians) and similar numbers of terms unique to the epistle but found in the New Testament outside of the Pauline corpus (84 in Ephesians, 90 [(80 if you subtract proper names] in Galatians).[20] Phrases we readily associate with Paul, such as "fruit of the Spirit" or "present evil age" or "the marks of Jesus," are found only in Galatians, but these are not used to disqualify that epistle as written by Paul. Instead, it is recognized that Paul's audience, the situation faced by Paul and the letter's recipients, as well as Paul's theological creativity and energy, all play a role in his choice of expression, style, and mood. Finally, some point to the expressions that serve to identify writers, much as a speaker's tone of voice and idiomatic turn of phrase serve to identify them. In particular, it is suggested that Ephesians has an unusually high number of the prepositions *kata* (according to or against) and *en* (in). However, Galatians actually uses *kata* with the genitive more than any other Pauline letter. Again, Romans uses *dia* (because of or through) and *para* (beside) more frequently, while Philippians prefers *meta* (after or with) and *peri* (around or concerning). Even more, Ephesians shares with Romans, Galatians, and 1 and 2 Thessalonians the special construction *ara . . . oun* (therefore . . . therefore).[21]

---

20. Ibid., 24.
21. Ibid., 28.

Relationship to Colossians

Not only are the literary character, the words chosen (or omitted), and the grammatical forms alleged to be outside Paul's expressive range, but the letter's similarity to Colossians raises red flags for many who believe the latter served as a model for the former. The argument concludes that Colossians as well as other letters of Paul was used in composing Ephesians. Both include a similar overall pattern and the household codes, both stress redemption, body, mystery, and power in similar ways, and both include exact parallel descriptions of Tychicus' instructions in delivering the letter. But these observations need not rule out Pauline authorship, for an examination of the data suggests that many of the similar terms include common prepositions, pronouns, and the words God and Christ. Again, scribes often made copies of their letters, in case the first was inadvertently destroyed or failed to make its destination. For example, Cicero remarks that his letter to Julius Caesar was ruined because the carrier managed to get it wet and the ink ran. But all was not lost, because Cicero had a copy of the letter, and so he re-sent it.[22] It was common to keep copies[23] and to share letters with friends, as does Cicero when he sends a copy of his letter to Pompey to Atticus.[24] It was assumed that people shared their letters, such that Cicero's friend Curius specifically asks Cicero *not* to show this particular letter to anyone.[25] And Cicero, Atticus, and others saved copies of what they wrote to use the text in other, similar circumstances. At one point Cicero blushes at this practice, for he admits that he used the same preface in two works. He clarifies that he was not paying attention when he sent the work in question to his friend Atticus, and it was only a bit later when he was reading another work that he saw it had the same preface. He explains that he keeps a volume of his prefaces from which he chooses suitable beginnings for his projects. In this case he was writing a new preface, and requests that Atticus cut out the old preface and glue the new one in place.[26]

Thus if Paul wrote Ephesians and Colossians within the same basic time frame, which fits with the note that Tychicus delivered both letters,

22. Cicero *Quint. fratr.* 2.11.4.
23. Cicero *Fam.* 7.25.1.
24. Cicero *Att.* 3.9.
25. Cicero *Fam.* 7.29.2.
26. Cicero *Att.* 16.6.

then one might comfortably assume Paul used the same scribe, and might have wished to stress similar ideas to churches in the same general region. Moreover, it seems ironic to declare that Ephesians is not by Paul because it uses language found in other Pauline material. Why assume a second author instead of asserting that the same author reused much of his material to address a similar circumstance? What is really at stake is not the vocabulary *per se*, but the alleged meaning of those terms. For that we turn in the next section to the theological arguments against Pauline authorship. In summary, the literary analysis does not show conclusively that Paul could not have written the epistle. Indeed, the evidence points to Pauline authorship inasmuch as it highlights the creativity of Paul to tailor his language to the audience and occasion. The number of *hapax legomena* or unique occurrences of terms in Ephesians are no more than we find in the undisputed letter to the Galatians, for example. Two options are left to consider: either Paul wrote the epistle which varied from his other letters by about 5 percent, or someone was able to match Paul's writing by 95 percent. These percentages suggest that Paul wrote Ephesians, but it is not on literary analysis alone that most render their judgments concerning Paul's authorship.

Theological Emphases in Ephesians

More troubling for many who argue a pseudepigraphic status for Ephesians are the theological and ideological statements permeating the letter that seem at odds with Pauline thought. For example, it is often said that Ephesians assumes a realized eschatology, with salvation having been accomplished fully in the past with no future implications (2:8–9). For example, Paul uses the perfect tense when speaking about believers being saved, rather than talking about the hope which looks forward. The cross is not emphasized, nor is justification; instead the exaltation of Christ and his cosmic superiority over all powers take center stage. Again, the emphasis on the church universal rather than the local body strikes many as deutero-Pauline. A closer look at the theology in Ephesians, however, suggests close connections with theology expressed in the undisputed letters. For example, although the term "cross" is found only once (2:16), this reference forms the platform upon which is built the arguments for reconciliation of humanity to God and between human groups (Jews and Gentiles). A similar case is made in 2 Cor 5:18–21 concerning reconciliation, where, interestingly, we also find Paul describing himself as God's ambassador, a term used in Eph 6:20 ("ambassador in chains"). Justification is a central concept in Romans and Galatians, but Paul does not use it in Colossians or the Thessalonian correspondence, and in 1 Corinthians the noun occurs only once (1:30), and the verb "to justify" twice (4:4, 6:11). The absence, then, of this particular word group should not disqualify Ephesians as Pauline. Additionally, the claim that Ephesians holds a realized eschatology fails to consider adequately both the future expectations noted in the epistle, as well as the use of the past tense by Paul in other letters when dealing with salvation. In 4:30, we find reference to the coming day of redemption, a future event (see also 1:10), as well as mention of the age to come in 1:21 and 2:7. Additionally, in Romans we discover Paul explaining the hope by which a believer is saved (past tense, 8:24) as well as declaring, also in the past tense, Christian brothers and sisters predestined, called, justified, and glorified (8:30). Speaking more broadly about eschatology, some suggest that in Ephesians Christ's imminent second coming has receded to the background, and shoved to the forefront is Paul's concern with the here and now. To substantiate this claim, the household code (Eph 5:21—6:9) is contrasted with 1 Cor 7:7 and Paul's encouragement later in 7:29–31 to refrain from marriage because the time is short. This contention, however, fails to appreciate fully the context of each argument. In 1 Corinthians, Paul faces a community struggling with issues of sexuality, and it seems that some married couples are refraining from sex with each other (7:1–5), although perhaps some husbands are visiting prostitutes (6:15–18). Moreover, the Corinthians downplayed the eschatological future in Christ, leaving Paul to insist upon it at every opportunity. Ephesians does not address sexual immorality or confusion within marriage; rather, it describes the institution in light of Christ and the church. And within the description is a forward looking emphasis, namely that the purpose of Christ's death was to make the church holy and blameless (see also 2 Cor 11:2). The church is not presently holy or blameless (at least as Paul describes the behaviors of believers in his letters!), but Paul is consistent with the larger New Testament picture of the church as the bride of Christ who, in the Last Day, will be presented to Christ (Matt 22:1–10; 25:1–13; Rev 19:7–10; 21:9). A final point concerning eschatology in Ephesians: Paul's command to put on the armor of God to fight against the powers and principalities (6:10–20) would be nonsensical if he believed that Christ had already defeated such powers, as some understand 1:20–22 to say. In Ephesians, as in the rest of the Pauline corpus, believers live in the tension between the now and the not yet; now is the time of salvation, but as of yet, not all that Christ has accomplished on the cross has been realized.

Finally, much has been made of the universal church described by Ephesians. Because Paul deals only with the local community in his other letters, so the argument contends, Ephesians must be deutero-Pauline. While it is true that Paul does not refer to the local church in Ephesians, it must also be stated that he does refer to the universal church in the uncontested letters. In 1 Corinthians, he addresses the letter not only to the local congregation but to all those everywhere who likewise call upon the name of the Lord Jesus (1 Cor 1:2). Moreover, he speaks to the Corinthians of baptism into one Spirit (1 Cor 12:7–14, see also Gal 3:27–9). The body of Christ is described as having various parts or dedicated ministries, such as apostles, prophets, teachers, and so on (12:27–31), with no hint that this configuration is based on the local church (a similar listing is found in Eph 4:11–13). In both Romans and Galatians, Paul speaks of believers as children of Abraham (Gal 3:29; Rom 4:16), clearly imagining a wide-reaching community. Lastly, as Paul describes his persecution of believers, he speaks of attacking the church of God, implying not isolated congregations but a larger group of communities (Gal 1:13; 1 Cor 15:9; Phil 3:6). Paul refers to the church as the "Israel of God" in Gal 6:16. Just as an individual synagogue would hardly imagine itself as other than part of the larger Jewish community, it appears that Paul too sees each congregation as connected to a larger entity, what he can refer to as the body of Christ (Eph 5:29; 1 Cor 12:13).

A final sticking point is Paul's declaration that the church is built on the apostles and prophets (Eph 2:20). This is said to conflict with his claim that the church's foundation is Christ (1 Cor 3:11, see also Col 2:7). But is there a sharp difference? Paul understands his apostolic ministry as speaking only of God's work in and through Christ, that is, the gospel and its ramifications. He is not at liberty to expand or eliminate any part of the tradition handed down to him. However, Paul should be given the flexibility to develop imagery that best describes the concepts, for his metaphors gain much of their power because they are dynamic. In Eph 2:20, Paul describes Christ Jesus as the chief cornerstone that secures the foundation of the building (the church), a sentiment not at all foreign to his point made to the Corinthians. In both cases, it is Christ who establishes the shape of the building and gives it security and strength.

Historical Context of Ephesians

A third area of concern for those who postulate Ephesians as pseudo-apostolic is the historical context of the letter, or more accurately, the apparent lack of historical context. In other letters, Paul is responding to intruders in the congregation (Galatians, 2 Corinthians), a letter sent by the community (1 Corinthians), a false teaching (Colossians), or even a gift sent by the community (Philippians). With Ephesians, nothing of the sort immediately presents itself. Additionally, alleged glimpses of the church suggest to some a congregation of a generation or more after Paul. Specifically, the church is described as fully integrated, with Jew and Gentile now one in the peace of Christ (2:14–18). Such a scene is markedly different from the tensions between Jew and Gentile that seem to permeate the Galatian churches or the Roman community. While these points have some merit, not all churches struggled with such tensions; for example, 1 and 2 Thessalonians as well as 1 and 2 Corinthians rarely mention the law or Jews or Judaism. It may be because the communities were mainly Gentile, but if Acts can be used to shed light here, we might suggest that some allied with the synagogue (Jews and God-fearers) began to associate with followers of Christ. Moreover, history does not support the assumption that a generation or two after Paul the church had sorted out the Jew/Gentile situation. Thus pushing the epistle into the second century does not help the problem. A close reading of Eph 2:11–21 suggests Paul is not describing the current state on the ground, as it were, in his congregation. Instead, he is declaring what the cross and resurrection have done to bring Gentiles, those formerly alienated from the true God, into fellowship with God's people (2:19). Indeed, it is precisely this truth that presents the historical setting for the epistle, namely the urgency for living out this unity within the congregations. And, we might add, interpreters have struggled to discern Paul's overarching reason for writing Romans (beyond his personal introduction and request for aid in his planned visit to Spain), but have accepted the letter as genuinely Pauline. Furthermore, the description of Paul in 3:1–11 raises problems for some. They note that the description of Paul as less than the least of the saints (3:8) is too harsh. Yet Paul describes himself elsewhere as one who was like an aborted fetus (1 Cor 15:8)—hardly a flattering picture. Others suggest that Paul would not identify apostles as holy (Eph 3:5), as this was a later, post-apostolic appellation. But Paul is quite complimentary when speaking of apostles as gifted by God (1 Cor 12:28). Could the same writer be both highly critical of Paul, and warmly sympathetic to the apostles (which included Paul, Eph 1:1)? Another problematic aspect of 3:1–11 is the apparent assumption by the author that the audience has not seen Paul, but has heard of him (see 3:1, which notes that they heard of Paul, implying that they did not know him directly). Presumably if Paul spent over two years in Ephesus (Acts 19:10), then many in that city would have known Paul personally. If this is an encyclical letter, however, then Paul could not assume that he has met with each of the churches who will hear this letter read in their congregations. A second possibility is to understand Paul's remarks as referring narrowly to his current imprisonment. If he is writing from Rome, the majority in Ephesus would be aware of his circumstances but not know them from personal encounter. Paul's point, then, in these verses would be to set his current situation in context: he is a prisoner for the sake of Gentiles (3:1) and rather than that news dismay or shame them, his sufferings are a source of glory for them (3:13). In sum, the biographical details of chapter 3 need not indicate an author other than Paul himself.

In conclusion, the results of the internal evidence point to including Ephesians as one of Paul's genuine letters, with the admitted distinctive language and content varying within an acceptable range from the undisputed letters. We proceed under the assumption that this letter was commissioned directly by Paul and was executed under his guidance and authority.

PSEUDONYMITY IN THE GRECO-ROMAN WORLD AND THE EARLY CHURCH

Historical Survey of Pseudonymity

Having examined much of the evidence put forward in support of understanding Ephesians as deutero-Pauline, a brief exploration of the notion of pseudonymity (borrowing a well-known author's name for one's own work) in the ancient world merits our attention. Until about 300 years ago, most readers of the Pauline corpus assumed all letters attributed to Paul were penned by him or his scribe. But with the rise of the modern criticism of the Bible, and a renewed interest in ancient literary practices, various scholars today assert that pseudonymity was an accepted and common literary convention in the ancient world. Some even assert that only four of Paul's epistles can be certified as genuine: Romans, 1 and 2 Corinthians, and Galatians. To evaluate these conclusions, several points should be taken up, including the nature of the claims about ancient pseudepigraphic letters, expectations of intellectual property, and the way the early church addressed pseudepigraphy and pseudonymity. We should note at the start that pseudepigraphic letters were popular in the Greco-Roman world, and Jews of this time also produced and read pseudepigraphic works. Both of these claims, however, require careful nuance if they are to inform the discussion over the authorship of Ephesians. When we think about the range of letters today, we imagine official letters sent between diplomats wherein every word is carefully parsed, as well as grade school children writing home from summer camp to parents or grandparents eager for some news (and perhaps in this latter case the contents would be likewise carefully edited!). In the ancient world, letters likewise served to unite friends, accomplish tasks, keep in touch with family, or simply entertain. In the latter category we find collections of letters presented as written by the ancient philosophers such as Plato (philosopher of the fourth century BCE who studied under Socrates) or Diogenes (Cynic philosopher of fourth-century BCE Athens). While no one doubts that the capabilities of those two men certainly extended to writing letters, the collections of their letters, produced in the Hellenistic period, were understood for the most part to be pseudepigraphic, that is, written by someone other than the claimed author. These collections served to entertain and edify, they offered another window into the imagined life of the great men (and a few women in their circles). Today they also are cited by some as an analogue to the deutero-Pauline material, so it is important that we explore the world of pseudonymity on the ancient landscape.

The definition of pseudonymity in modern scholarship varies widely, at times being conflated with the category of "anonymous." A genuine letter is one written (directly or indirectly through a scribe) or commissioned by the author named in the text. An anonymous letter does not contain within the text an attribution to authorship; however, such a text might later have an author falsely attributed to it. For our purposes, a pseudepigraphic letter is one written by a person other than the one named in the text, and thus the text's author could be categorized as pseudonymous. A key concern when speaking of pseudonymity is the intention of the authors; namely, are they intending to deceive their audience, or are they using an accepted literary device? Intentions are not always easy to determine, but two were commented upon in the ancient world: greed and admiration for the author. Some writers were anxious to have their own ideas propagated, and so used a well-known name to forward the writer's cause, while others genuinely appreciated the person whose name they used, and sought to promote that person's ideas out of love, respect, and personal humility. Forgery is another category; here the author intentionally deceives his audience for some perceived gain, which might be wealth, or the downfall of his opponent. In the case of pseudonymous authorship, the audience is not deceived; rather it recognizes without censure the false authorship attribution.

A quick summary of the pseudepigraphic epistolary collections in the Greco-Roman world reveals that they were the product of several authors, or at least an accumulation of material surrounding an authentic core. These collections developed in the first and second centuries CE, perhaps because of the general, widespread interest in classical Greek thought and literary expression. The figures chosen had well-known reputations, and the letter collections might be read alongside their corpus of work. In almost all cases the letters were written to a single individual, another well-known person of the past. Moreover, composing letters in the name of famous philosophers, tyrants, and kings was standard rhetoric training for students. "The goal of the pseudonymous epistolographer was thus to work the bare bones of a biography into a compelling life story. He was both scholar and creative artist, researching historical materials in order to define the bounds of the tradition, and using his imagination to elaborate creatively and dramatically on that tradition."[27] It must be noted that these letters were not read singly, but within the corpus, and the evidence suggests a school setting for their production. For these reasons, a few argued that the disputed Pauline letters were produced by a Pauline school, although this view has never gained much traction due to the paucity of evidence for such an academy.

Additionally, many of these collections focus on ethics and imitating the famous figure. To facilitate these goals, often the letters include person-

27. Rosenmeyer 2001: 198–99.

al data or alleged historical details that might motivate the reader to copy the philosopher's behavior. Since the reader knew the important figure of the distant past was not in fact the author, presenting the personal details as though the philosopher himself wrote it was not deceptive, but rather a literary convention that served to promote the well-known ideals of the philosophy. Because genuine letters can exhibit similar characteristics, such as encouraging imitation and stressing ethics, recognizing pseudepigraphic epistles is not, therefore, always simple and straightforward.

Pausing for a moment, it seems useful to ask whether the characteristics noted above are helpful in deciding whether there are pseudepigraphic letters in the New Testament. A review of the various Greco-Roman corpuses reveals few similarities with the Pauline corpus. Many in the former category do not have the sender's name in each letter; rather, the real reader knows who the sender is because the letter is embedded in the larger corpus of epistles attributed to that figure. Second, often the material is of a very general nature, amounting to a philosophical reflection. Third, the letters are usually much shorter than the ones in the New Testament, though a few are the length of Paul's shorter letters. Finally, the attributed author is a figure from the distant, classical Greek period. An exception is the second-century CE collection of Apollonius of Tyana's letters, which, as single-line statements or quips, are hardly comparable to the epistles of the New Testament.

Authority and Ownership of Literary "Property"

Digging deeper into the issue of ancient pseudepigraphy requires an examination into the sense of intellectual property held at the time, and the role of the apostle and apostolic authority within the early church. While no copyright law existed in the ancient world (that would not happen until the advent of the printing press), there were guidelines and standards of behavior. Readers held a much more *laissez-faire* attitude towards fictitious letters by Plato, and reacted strongly against letters reportedly by Cicero but written by another. The rule of thumb was that if the alleged author is long deceased, and his ideas and thoughts had been widely disseminated and absorbed, then producing letters to help an audience understand the great man's personal life and ideas was considered acceptable. As noted above, letter collections of Plato, Diogenes and other Cynic philosophers, or Pythagoras (sixth-century BCE philosopher and mathematician) and the Neo-Pythagoreans, were usually produced by a school, or at least several hands are evident in the final redaction. Indeed, ancient commentators pointed out that Pythagoras was known to have written little himself, but much of his surviving work is the result of his disciples' careful note taking. For example, Porphyry (second-century CE Neoplatonist) notes that of the 280 works with Pythagoras' name attached, only 80 are from the philosopher directly; the others were written by his disciples. This fact was not troubling because, as Iamblichus (Neoplatonist, ca. 250–325 CE) observes, it was their custom to sign everything in their master's name. Olympiodorus (sixth-century CE Neoplatonist) notes that Pythagoras did not leave any personal writings behind because he believed his "spiritual" writings, his disciples, were a better source for hearing his philosophy. These students out of goodwill for their esteemed teacher wrote down his teachings from their notes. Pythagoras is thus somewhat distinctive in that he chose not to write but instructed his students to do so. We have no record of Paul making a similar request, and of course, Paul also wrote some letters. But if someone wrote in Cicero's name, or Seneca's, they faced condemnation, because the purpose of writing such a letter was either the real author's personal gain or the disgrace of the important figure. The physician Galen (second century CE) laments that his works were redacted in inappropriate and lazy ways that violated his literary property. He wrote *On His Own Books* in an attempt to stem the tide of these inferior works, wherein he recounts an incident that highlights his frustration over forgeries and unscrupulous editors. He explains that a group had gathered in a bookshop and was discussing the authenticity of one of his books. A fellow steps forward, reads the first couple of lines, and tosses it aside as fake, because it was evident that it was not Galen's style.[28] Likewise Quintilian says he published only one of his court orations; however, to his great dismay, the court stenographers, having recorded what was said, later took his ideas and expressed them in their own words.[29] Quintilian felt he should have the rights to publish his spoken word, that his orations were not part of public domain.

What troubled these authors and others was not simply that someone might gain financially from this deception, but that the entire corpus of their work, their ideas and reputation, could be smeared or lowered

---

28. Metzger 1972: 6.
29. Quintilian *Inst.* 7.2.24.

with the addition of works claiming to be their own. Herodotus explains that Onomacritus was exiled from Athens for adding to the oracles of Musaeus.[30] Diogenes Laertius notes that the Stoic Diotimus wrote fifty obscene letters in his opponent Epicurus' name, attempting to ruin his reputation.[31] But notice also in Galen's story above that at least some ancient readers asked questions of authorship by examining the style of a work compared to known authentic texts. Suetonius echoes the same sentiment in his critique of some works in the Homer corpus that he identifies as not genuine because they are both common and obscure, that is, their style and grammar did not match that of the genuine works of Homer. "What emerges clearly is the widespread use of pseudonymity in Greco-Roman antiquity, a literary practice well-regarded by some but held in contempt by others."[32]

Plato's Noble Falsehood

Alongside the question of intellectual property is Plato's concept of a noble falsehood. The idea taught that if a fabrication would help a person, then it was acceptable for someone to tell a lie. The example often given by the ancient authors themselves was of a physician who, in order to help the patient, would lie about a remedy so that the patient would follow orders and thus be healed. Some argue that the early church would have accepted a pseudepigraphic letter if its content was in line with apostolic thought, because the message mattered more than the medium. While it is true that a few church fathers speak favorably of the noble falsehood, the contexts differ so greatly from the issues of apostolic writings so as to limit their usefulness in the argument. For example, Chrysostom approves of the noble falsehood, but the context is his "lie" to his friend concerning their joining the priesthood.[33] He explains why he was not straightforward about his own actions in the matter, but notes that he obfuscated his position for his friend's greater good. Again, Origen admits that the noble falsehood is a logically conceivable way of understanding

---

30. Herodotus *Hist.* 7.6.
31. Diogenes Laertius *Lives* 10.3.
32. Clarke 2002: 452.
33. John Chrysostom *Sac.* 1.8.

how Jesus might have taught.[34] But he then goes on to reject that possibility as it pertains to Christ. Finally, Clement of Alexandria uses the concept, even citing the example similar to the one noted above of a physician's practice.[35] He suggests that such was also used by Paul in circumcising Timothy, but in the end he says that he cannot accept the label of deceit; Paul was accommodating to the Jewish sensibilities, not being deceitful. Interestingly, Chrysostom, in his long explanation to his friend about his apparent duplicity, also notes Paul's circumcision of Timothy, and likewise rejects a label of deception. In any case, while these few church fathers do acknowledge the noble falsehood as a possible reality in their daily lives, they do not accept it as the *modus operandi* for apostles and Jesus Christ. It seems, then, that the early believers would not have countenanced a pseudepigraphic letter on the grounds it that was a noble falsehood.

Evidence from the Early Church

The early church resisted accepting as authoritative anything beyond the apostolic period, such as the *Acts of Paul*.[36] For example, in the fifth century, the presbyter Salvian wrote *Timothei ad Ecclesiam* (*libri IV*). The local bishop guessed that his presbyter was responsible, and protested the writing. Salvian responded that he knew who wrote it (he denied responsibility), and that he felt it necessary to attach an authoritative name to the work, for otherwise no one would read it. Moreover, Salvian asserted the author was being humble by not attaching his name. And anyway, the name Timothy was chosen as a play on words, for it means "honor of God." Salvian wanted it both ways, to say that people read it because of the reputed author, and that the name means nothing. At bottom, Salvian (the likely author) used the name Timothy to deceive the readers, and his bishop denounced it. The problem is addressed from a different angle in Eusebius' discussion of Dionysius, bishop of Corinth (ca. 170 CE), who commented that his epistles had been defaced. "As the brethren desired me to write epistles, I wrote. And these epistles the apostles of the devil have filled with tares, cutting out some things and adding others. For

34. Origen *Cels.* 4.19.

35. Clement of Alexandria *Strom.* 7.53.

36. The issues surrounding the rejection of the *Acts of Paul* are complex, but in the mix is the belief that it was written in the second century, after the apostolic period, and thus not meriting the highest level of authority within the church.

them a woe is reserved. It is, therefore, not to be wondered at if some have attempted to adulterate the Lord's writings also, since they have formed designs even against writings which are of less account."[37]

One might argue that such late evidence does not help us with Ephesians, which is an early work. In an interesting twist, some scholars have suggested that the earliest church followed the Jewish practice of accepting pseudepigraphic works, and that second-century Gentile Christians condemned the practice.[38] Some of the Jewish pseudepigraphic texts cited to defend the theory, however, are from the apocalyptic genre, which might as part of its literary technique attribute the text to a worthy ancient such as Enoch or Ezra. The Christian biblical texts were written in the apostolic age and use apostles' names, not names of the distant past. Additionally, 1 Baruch and its final chapter, the Epistle of Jeremiah, while part of the LXX and the Vulgate, were not included in the Jewish canon. It is difficult, then, to state definitively from this example that Jews accepted pseudepigraphy. The Epistle of Jeremiah does not begin with the sender's salutation, but the narrator indicates that this was a letter the prophet sent to the exiles in Babylon. The lack of salutation limits its usefulness as a direct comparison to Ephesians. Generally speaking, the pseudepigraphic works use the names of ancient patriarchs or heroes of the faith, which increases the possibility that the Jewish authors mirrored the Gentile writers. Both looked back with admiration at their historical past, and wished to have those great figures speak anew in their day. We might bring the book of Hebrews into the discussion here. This work was ultimately put into the Christian canon by connecting it with the Apostle Paul, though the letter itself is anonymous. Origen's discussion of Hebrews is instructive. He recognizes that the style of speech is much better than Paul's rough wording. But he also observes that the content is Pauline, and suggests that someone who was very familiar with Paul's ideas, who perhaps even took notes from the master, wrote the piece. Origen acknowledges that those who claim it comes from Paul are right to say so. But as for him, he declines to make any specific judgment, instead admitting that only God knows who wrote it. That does not stop him quoting Hebrews as though it were Paul's work.[39] From this evidence two points should be empha-

---

37. Eusebius *Hist. eccl.* 4.23.12.
38. Bauckham 1983: 162.
39. Origen *Princ.* 3.1.10; 3.2.4; *Cels.* 7.29.

sized. First, Origen was well aware of the Greek style and grammar of the Pauline corpus, and was comfortable discussing questions of authenticity based on that data. Second, Origen does not say anything similar about the disputed Pauline epistles as he does about Hebrews. That is, he does not offer that the style, grammar, or theology of any of the Pauline letters might have been that of a disciple of Paul who used Paul's name to extend Paul's thought for a new day or situation.

A related issue is that of apostolic authority. Paul insists that his apostolic authority is of a special type: it is directly from God (Gal 1:1). We have no evidence that Paul seconded that authority to his coworkers; indeed, that would not be possible, for only God could appoint apostles (1 Cor 12:4, 28). And the early church also regarded the era of the apostles, and the apostles themselves, as divinely commissioned to communicate the word of God. Yet Hebrews shows that authoritative material need not have within its text the name of an apostle (the canonical Gospels are another example; the author's name is found in the title page). What does seem off limits is assuming apostolic authority without having been given that responsibility by God.[40]

Conclusion

In closing, I justify the time spent reviewing the evidence concerning pseudonymity in the Greco-Roman world and early church because the issue is often treated as a *fait accompli*: the Ephesians letter is pseudepigraphic, but not deceptive both because the early church accepted the wider conventions of pseudonymity, and because the ancients had little sense of intellectual property. This survey has cautioned against accepting these claims. Instead, the evidence suggests the church did not accept (knowingly) pseudepigraphic letters or works. If Ephesians is determined to be pseudepigraphic, then the use of Paul's name and personal data were included in an effort to pass off the letter as genuine. In that case, it was an attempt, in the end successful, to deceive the audience.[41] This conclusion must then be processed with issues of canon (a difficult subject in its own right) and of apostolic authority.

40. Brevard Childs (1994: 52) argues, however, that the authority of the biblical text comes from its status as canon, not its authorship.

41. Wilder 2004: 250.

PAUL'S IMPRISONMENT

Proceeding under the conviction that Paul wrote Ephesians, we turn our attention to the significance of Paul's imprisonment as the backdrop to this letter. Two locations are generally given as the setting for the writing: Ephesus and Rome (with a small minority suggesting Caesarea Maritima). Acts notes Paul's imprisonment in Rome (and Caesarea Maritima) and Paul makes a comment about facing beasts in Ephesus, which some suggest is an oblique reference to an imprisonment there (1 Cor 15:32). The resolution of this problem is controlled in part by conclusions reached concerning Pauline authorship of Philemon and Colossians, and to a lesser extent, Philippians. Put simply, the problem involves *four* epistles (known as the prison epistles), *three* interconnected lists of names, *two* very similar epistles (Ephesians and Colossians), and *one* author, Paul. It seems that Paul was in the same location when he composed Philemon and Colossians, because Timothy coauthored the letters and so many of the same people are referenced in both letters, including the slave Onesimus. Additionally, it seems that Paul was in the same location when he wrote Ephesians and Colossians, because both were to be delivered by the same person, Tychicus. That suggests a scenario that allows for a single imprisonment for at least three of the four prison epistles.[42]

Onesimus' Status

A key element in the debate is the role played by Onesimus, Philemon's slave. The general consensus has been that Onesimus was a runaway slave who happened upon Paul while both were imprisoned, and there he came to faith in Christ through Paul's ministry. Following this fortuitous outcome, Paul seeks Onesimus' release from Philemon, his owner and Paul's friend. Decisions about where Paul is imprisoned when he writes to Philemon are thus predicated on where one imagines a runaway slave might flee, or more specifically, how far might he travel from Colossae. The events are reconstructed as follows: Onesimus is imprisoned with Paul and becomes a follower of Christ. Paul is duty bound to send Onesimus back to Philemon, but he urgently desires that Philemon free his slave. He urges Philemon to settle the outstanding debts owed by Onesimus to

---

42. Second Timothy also claims to be written from prison, but it is grouped with 1 Tim and Titus in the Pastoral Epistles.

Paul's account. The letter is a success; Philemon frees Onesimus, who returns to Paul who is still imprisoned. After some unspecified time elapses, Tychicus and Onesimus return to Colossae with their letter (and presumably the one to the Laodiceans).

The above scenario depends upon Onesimus being a runaway slave, but such a conclusion has rightly come under heavy scrutiny in recent years. First, it assumes that runaway slaves were imprisoned, but why did the person who captured Onesimus not return him to his owner, especially as often rewards were given for returned slaves? Second, it is alleged that Onesimus stole from Philemon, but Paul does not include any mention of Onesimus' repentance for running away or stealing goods. In fact, Paul does not even mention that he had found Philemon's runaway slave! This suggests that Philemon knew Onesimus' location and was aware of his reason for being there.

Another theory suggests that Onesimus was not so much running away as seeking out Paul to mediate a disagreement between himself and Philemon. The argument draws on the figure of the *amicus domini*, or friend of the master. An ancient example from the early second century CE often cited is Pliny the Younger's letter to his friend Sabinianus.[43] In this exchange, Pliny speaks of Sabinianus' freedman (a *former* slave) who begs Sabinianus' mercy and forgiveness by beseeching Pliny to speak on his behalf. Pliny agrees, and writes to assure his friend Sabinianus that the freedman is reformed, repentant of his past deeds, and ready to make a clean start. None of these details are present, however, in Paul's letter to Philemon. Moreover, no mention is made of Onesimus repenting and seeking mercy, or of Philemon being angry at his slave's behavior (Pliny notes Sabinianus' outrage at his freedman's behavior). Importantly, Pliny is speaking about a freed slave, not one currently enslaved.

A second, and stronger, argument concerning Onesimus is that he was sent to Paul by Philemon to help the former survive in prison. Onesimus was functioning in a similar way to Epaphroditus, who was the emissary for the Philippian church, bringing aid and cheer to the confined apostle (Phil 2:25). Onesimus apparently became quite valuable to Paul's ongoing ministry, thus prompting Paul to ask that Philemon consider releasing Onesimus to full-time service with Paul. This reconstruction makes better sense of Paul's letter to Philemon, and is more historically

---

43. Pliny the Younger *Ep.* 9.21.

sensitive to the situation of ancient slavery and the realities of imprisonment. A close examination of the letter reveals language commonly used
in speaking about letter carriers and private messengers. Specifically, Paul
implies that he would rather not send back Onesimus at that particular
moment (12–14), suggesting that Onesimus was permitted by Philemon
to stay only a specified amount of time.[44] Moreover, Paul uses the verb
anapempō (to send back) in v. 12, which is often used in correspondence
to signify the return of the messenger.[45]

In the end, it does seem to defy the odds that Onesimus, a runaway
slave, would be imprisoned with Paul, especially in a city as large as
Ephesus or Rome. Paul, as a Roman citizen, would not suffer the same
fate as a slave, even in prison. Acts 16:22–24 records Paul's chains and
imprisonment in the deepest recesses of the Philippian jail, and notes that
this treatment was unacceptable for a Roman citizen who had not yet
been condemned. The situation was resolved with an apology by the city
council (16:37–39). Again, why would Paul believe he had authority to
decide whether to return Onesimus to his owner? Surely once his status
was known, would not Onesimus be returned irrespective of Paul's own
thoughts on the subject? Paul was chained to Roman guards; it seems
unlikely that they would have turned a blind eye to a runaway slave helping their captive.

It must be noted as well that in the Roman period, a freed slave was
still beholden to his owner, under the latter's power, much as a father
retained authority over his grown children. It would not be enough, then,
for Onesimus to be granted freedom, Philemon must also release him to
serve Paul and the ministry. Paul's letter requesting as much fits this reconstruction of events. Finally, if one assumed that Onesimus was fleeing
his owner, either as a runaway or as one seeking a mediator, then a more
cynical (but possible) reading of his situation was that he agreed to the
gospel message only to enhance his standing with Paul. One might argue
that Philemon (and Paul) would suspect the genuineness of Onesimus's
conversion, inasmuch as his profession of faith was a key argument for his
release and forgiveness of all past deeds and debts. But if Philemon sent
Onesimus to Paul, the genuineness of the latter's conversion is on more
solid ground.

44. Wansink 1996: 189–91.
45. See *1 Clem.* 65.1; Josephus *J.W.* 2.207, 450; idem *Ant.* 16.293.

Ephesus Imprisonment

Looking closely at the arguments for Paul's imprisonment in Ephesus, one assertion put forward depends on Onesimus's runaway status. The claim is that he would not have had the funds to flee to Rome. This theory usually alleges that he stole from Philemon, which invites the question of why Onesimus did not steal enough to get himself as far from Colossae as possible. Where better to lose oneself than in Rome, a city of a million people, as some estimates put Rome's population in the first century CE? A second argument in favor of an Ephesus imprisonment focuses on accommodating the several visits between Colossae and Paul indicated by the correspondence. The timeline runs as follows: Onesimus meets Paul, Paul sends a letter with Onesimus back to Philemon, the latter frees Onesimus to serve with Paul (who is in prison), and Tychicus is sent with Onesimus back to Colossae. Travel between Ephesus and Colossae is about five days; between Colossae and Rome about two months. Thus it would be quite simple for Philemon to send Onesimus to care for Paul in Ephesus, and for the former to make several trips back to Colossae.

A serious challenge to the Ephesus theory is the lack of evidence for an Ephesus imprisonment. Acts is silent on this, which in and of itself does not disqualify the argument. But the positive evidence is likewise slim. Paul speaks of enduring many imprisonments (2 Cor 11:23), and specifically of facing "wild beasts in Ephesus" (1 Cor 15:32). This latter phrase is taken as implying some sort of literal incarceration in the city. Several points, however, caution against drawing this conclusion. First, if Paul was given over literally to the beasts, he would have been stripped of his citizenship. However, from Acts it appears that Paul retained his citizenship throughout his ministry. Moreover, the content in 1 Cor 15 has many connections with the philosophical jargon of the day. Often philosophers would speak of battling their passions and hedonistic rivals with language similar to Paul. Paul quotes from the philosopher Menander, "Bad company corrupts good character" (15:32), which suggests he is placing his argument in the context of a philosopher's admonitions. Moreover, Paul uses the diatribe method, firing off rhetorical questions to jar the Corinthians back to their senses and act rightly.[46] This form of argumentation was common among philosophers.

---

46. Malherbe 1989: 80–89.

Finally, we must raise the obvious question: Why would Paul send a letter to the Ephesians, or even to satellite churches surrounding Ephesus, if he was imprisoned in their midst? Or from another angle, if he was unable to speak with the Ephesian Christians, one would presume that he would lack the liberty to write to them. Either way, if Paul was in an Ephesus jail, it seems highly unlikely that he would choose to write to the church in that very same city. Indeed those who postulate an Ephesus locale for Colossians and Philemon generally suggest a Rome venue for Ephesians, precisely because it is so difficult to explain why Paul would write when he could presumably speak directly with the Ephesian church. The similar statements in Ephesians and Colossians about Tychicus delivering the letters are usually explained as the author of Ephesians copying from Paul's letter to the Colossians.

Rome Imprisonment

That leaves Rome as the most likely spot for Paul's imprisonment in composing the four prison epistles. The major roadblock raised against this theory is the length of time it would take to make a journey from Rome to Philippi, Ephesus, or Colossae. At this point we should note that Philippi and Ephesus were major cities in themselves; Ephesus was the largest and most important city in Asia Minor, and Philippi was a Roman colony. Thus travel between these cities and Rome by all manner of traders, government officials, and military personnel would have been frequent. Assuming the typical distance of 15–20 miles per day on foot, it would take the average traveler from Rome to Philippi about two or three weeks to traverse the 360 miles to the eastern Italian port city of Brundisium, then two days to sail to Greece (perhaps the port cities of Dyrrachium or Aulona), with the final 370 miles of the journey along the Via Egnatia (the superhighway of the day) to Philippi taking about another two weeks. The 800 miles could be covered in about a month and a half. Alternatively, Paul's envoy traveling to Ephesus might take a boat from Italy to Corinth, then on to Ephesus. This route would take one to two weeks from Rome to Corinth, and then another week to Ephesus, but so much depended upon the winds.[47] The time involved, then, in traveling to Rome from either Ephesus or Philippi was not appreciably more than traveling on

47. Casson 1994: 150–52.

foot between the two latter cities. Hence a Roman imprisonment seems the most likely provenance for the letter to the Ephesians.

DATE OF EPHESIANS

Assuming Paul wrote from Rome, we can then date the letter to the early 60s CE. The first letter he wrote would be to Philemon. This might have been written within a few months of his arrival at Rome. After Onesimus returned to Rome (which might take as little as two and a half months), Paul set about writing to the Colossians and the Ephesians. We might suggest that Paul wrote these in late 60 or early 61. This date takes into account the earthquake that hit nearby Laodicea. Tacitus explains that, though it was devastated, Laodicea rebuilt quickly and without Rome's financial assistance. Because no mention of such a natural disaster is noted by Paul, many argue Colossians could not have been written after the tragedy. Alternatively, since we do not have Paul's letter to the Laodiceans, we have no way of knowing whether Paul was writing to encourage the church as they faced the catastrophe. However, Paul made no mention of the expulsion of Jews from Rome under Claudius in his later letter to the Romans, so we need not assume that major social or natural upheavals would be so noted in Paul's letters. Arguably he might have considered such a note redundant or obvious. Thus, while a date in early 61 would work, it is unclear whether we should accommodate the date of the earthquake when determining the writing of Colossians and Ephesians. And while these movements are taking place, Paul is also communicating with the Philippian church, with Epaphroditus serving as their envoy conveying aid and service to Paul.

AUDIENCE OF EPHESIANS

A major hurdle in describing the community (or communities) receiving this letter is that the church described is universal. Moreover, if we take Ephesians as an encyclical letter, we are left to surmise which satellite towns received the letter. While I argue that Ephesus is the most likely target for the letter, the possibility of several outlying churches receiving it is quite strong. In either case, the fact that Paul speaks of the church not as a local body but in its universal dimensions means that we must look to topics in the letter which pertain to the general social world in reconstructing the recipients. Such an approach is similar to 1 Peter, James, or Hebrews, letters whose addressees are unspecified in terms of a city. Judging by the content of the letter itself, several tentative conclusions can be drawn about the audience receiving this letter. Unlike his tension-filled letter to the Galatians, in this epistle Paul is comfortable with the congregation. They are on good terms, and Paul feels his time among them has been effective (1 Cor 16:9). But that does not mean that Paul's time in Ephesus was one long holiday. Paul informs the Corinthians of serious struggles and suffering he endured in Ephesus, and Acts describes the riot that flared up surrounding Paul's teaching and healing. It seems probable that the Ephesian Christians faced similar hostility, though not of the same magnitude. Both the Philippian and the Thessalonian churches faced serious persecutions, and Acts indicates that Paul was persecuted harshly in both cities. The same pattern likely existed in Ephesus.

First Corinthians gives us a window into at least a few members of the Ephesian church. Paul wrote 1 Corinthians from Ephesus (1 Cor 16:8) and his coauthor was Sosthenes (1 Cor 1:1). Was this the same person who in Acts was a leader in the synagogue in Corinth? The fact that Paul offers no introduction beyond the label "brother" suggests that Sosthenes was well known to the Corinthians, lending weight to the conclusion that this person met Paul in Corinth, and traveled with him to Ephesus. Paul notes that some people from Chloe reported divisions within the Corinthian church. We know precious little about these people, or Chloe for that matter. The strongest suggestion is that they were outsiders to the local Christian community because they brought what Paul evaluates as unbiased information. We could reasonably surmise that Chloe's people (and perhaps Chloe herself) were members of the Ephesian church. In the final chapter he mentions Timothy coming to the Corinthians, presumably from Ephesus. He also notes the presence of Apollos, who was not anxious to travel to Corinth in the immediate future, and we might assume that he remained in Ephesus. From 2 Cor 2:4 and 7:6–11 we learn that Titus was with Paul in Ephesus, and took his "tearful" letter to them. Finally Paul makes special mention of Aquila and Priscilla and the church meeting in their home in 1 Cor 16:19. This Jewish couple is described in Acts (18:2) as originally coming to Corinth from Rome (being expelled under Emperor Claudius). Paul shared their profession (tent making or leather working), and lived with them. After eighteen months, all three left Corinth and headed to Ephesus, where it appears the couple remained for some years.

We find them mentioned again by Paul in his letter to the Romans (16:3–4). This curiosity has prompted the theory that Rom 16 was actually sent to the Ephesians, perhaps as a letter of recommendation for Phoebe, the deacon of Cenchreae. Textual evidence is called upon to support this theory: the earliest copy of Romans (P[46]) includes chapter 16 after the doxology of 16:25–27, for example, suggesting the names were attached by a later copyist. If this reconstruction is accurate, then we have a decidedly clearer picture of some who populated the Ephesian church. However, serious doubts are raised, including that every ancient manuscript contains the listing. And we have every reason to suppose that Priscilla and Aquila, with Claudius's edict rescinded, returned to Rome along with many of their Jewish compatriots. In Paul's other letters to churches he started, he does not offer a list of people to receive his greetings (see Galatians, Philippians, 1 and 2 Thessalonians, 1 and 2 Corinthians). Would someone in Ephesus feel snubbed if Paul forgot (or declined) to mention them by name? Instead, it seems most likely that the list of names in Rom 16:1–16 was intended for Rome, an opportunity for Paul to connect with the wider community by noting that he has friends and acquaintances among them.[48]

The Ephesian letter recipients line up with the social patterns of the larger Greco-Roman culture. They are members of families: slaves or masters, parents, spouses. They seem to be neither wealthy nor destitute; indeed, their financial status is not addressed directly. A sizable number, perhaps the majority, are Gentile, for Paul speaks of himself and other Jews as "we" and the letter's recipients as "you" Gentiles. This distinction remains crucial for Paul's argument concerning the advantages wrought in Christ, namely that through his death he made the two groups one in the church. Yet it also appears that some members of his ministry team working in Ephesus were Jewish, including Aquila, Priscilla, Timothy, Apollos, and perhaps Sosthenes.

---

48. Das 2007, 16–23.

THE CITY OF EPHESUS IN PAUL'S DAY

The mixture of Jew and Gentile revealed in Paul's letter mirrored the larger social context. Josephus informs us that a sizable Jewish population of 2000 families was resettled in this region by the Seleucids in the late third century BCE.[49] Probably some moved to Ephesus and established their families and businesses. Jews in Ephesus were permitted to practice their ancestral customs, although the latter half of the first century BCE included disputes with the Gentile leadership in the city. At the end of the first century BCE, Augustus established that Jews could follow their own laws and customs, could send money and donations to Jerusalem, and were excused from appearing in court on the Sabbath. Jews with Roman citizenship were exempt from military service. In Paul's day, Jews and Gentiles apparently interacted with equanimity. Despite the fact that a synagogue has not been excavated in Ephesus, both Josephus and the book of Acts informs us of Jews meeting together.[50]

The population of Ephesus likely numbered 200,000 to 250,000 in the first century CE, making it the third largest city in the Roman Empire (Rome and Alexandria took first and second place).[51] The city had much to offer its inhabitants. It was located strategically at the mouth of the Cayster River on the eastern coast of the Aegean Sea, providing easy transport of goods and people into and out of western Asia Minor. In 31 BCE Ephesus was named the capital of the Roman province of Asia, and within two years it included an imperial temple dedicated to Roma and the divine Julius Caesar. Wealth poured into the city, providing the resources to build magnificent temples, monuments, fountains, theaters, baths, and houses. A visitor today can walk the lengthy paved main street lined with elaborately carved columns and arches, remains of its glory days. Terrace houses built into the hillside retain their beautiful mosaic and fresco interior decorations, attesting to the affluence of this ancient city. In the 50s and 60s CE, Ephesians might be entertained in the grand theater, which seated 25,000, or visit public baths and the gymnasium. The exalted reputation of ancient Ephesus lay primarily in its magnificent temple to Artemis. One of the seven wonders of the ancient world, it was about four times larger than the Parthenon in Athens, making it the largest

49. Josephus *Ant.* 12.148–53.
50. Ibid., 14.227; Acts 18:19, 26; 19:8–9.
51. Trebilco 2004: 17.

Greek temple in the ancient world. Poets praised its unmatched splendor, including Antipater of Sidon who, comparing the temple to the hanging gardens of Babylon, the colossus, and the pyramids of Egypt, declared "but when I saw the house of Artemis that mounted to the clouds, those other marvels lost their brilliancy, and I said, 'Lo, apart from Olympus, the Sun never looked on aught so grand.'"[52] Sadly today, all that is left of its former majesty is a single column providing a nesting place for birds.

52. Murphy-O'Connor 2008: 160.

EPHESIANS 1

The opening chapter of Ephesians is richly laced with superlatives, rhetorical flourishes, and repetition of ideas that all serve to magnify God the Trinity. After identifying himself and the letter's recipients, Paul launches into a ten-verse eulogy praising God the Father and his work of salvation through the Messiah and the fulfilled promises through the Holy Spirit. Hard on the heels of the eulogy is Paul's thanksgiving, reflecting a natural response of prayer that believers might most fully understand and know the God spoken of in the blessing. The eulogy begins with the note that God has blessed us with every spiritual blessing, and the thanksgiving ends with acknowledging that Christ's body, the church, is filled with the fullness of the one (Christ) who fills all things. Paul employs a similar strategy in 2 Corinthians, which begins with a eulogy, opening with the same line, praising the God and Father of our Lord Jesus Christ. Perhaps it is no coincidence that Paul begins 2 Corinthians with praise, for he recounts that he faced terrible circumstances in the recent past, such that he feared he might die. It takes little imagination to suggest that Paul in writing Ephesians contemplated his own death while imprisoned in Rome. It is a testimony to his convictions that in both 2 Corinthians and Ephesians his response was praise. Acts 16:24–25 relays Paul and Silas' prison worship of songs and prayers, further supporting the picture that when Paul was in dire straits, his instinct was to praise God. Moreover, in Ephesians as in his other letters, Paul uses the thanksgiving to introduce important ideas developed later in the epistle. In this case we find faith, love, and hope rooted in the Father, the Lord Jesus, and the Spirit, as well as the believers' knowledge and wisdom, and Christ's surpassing power in this age and the next.

SALUTATION (1:1–2)

> [1]Paul, an apostle of Christ Jesus by the will of God, to God's
> holy people in Ephesus, the faithful in Christ Jesus: [2]Grace
> and peace to you from God our Father and the Lord Jesus
> Christ.

Paul identifies himself as the only author of the letter. In this Ephesians
is similar to Romans and Galatians. It is a bit curious here, inasmuch as
Timothy is a coauthor in Colossians, Philippians, and Philemon. However,
Ephesians is similar to Romans in that Paul is writing to at least some
people who are unknown personally to him. Paul identifies himself as an
apostle of Christ Jesus by the will of God; this is the exact same phrase
used in 2 Cor 1:1, but similar language is used generally in Paul's saluta-
tions. Paul follows normal letter protocol, wherein the sender is identified at the beginning, as well as the recipients. In Ephesians, they are the
saints or holy ones, also a general moniker used by Paul for those who are
believers. The term "saints" or "holy people" has come to mean only a se-
lect few who have lived exemplary lives and are canonized by the church.
What does it say about Paul's understanding of the work of the cross that
he would call any believer a saint or holy one? We can say at least that this
is an identity believers share; it is a result of their being in Christ. In 1:4,
the same term is used in conjunction with "blameless" to describe those
who are chosen by God through Jesus Christ. The term "holy ones" is
used in three ways in the New Testament: it describes a spiritual community of holy members (1 Cor 6:2), indicates personal sanctification (1 Pet
1:15–16), or, predominantly, distinguishes the local or visible Christian
community made up of believers (Rom 1:7, 15:26, 1 Cor 1:2). In Eph 1:1,
the latter definition seems likely, but 1:4 could arguably suggest personal
sanctification, especially if Paul's point is individual election (see below).
Again, it may be that 1:4 describes the future of believers, as ones holy and
blameless (see also 5:27). Of course, these ideas are not mutually exclusive
in as much as Paul could imagine that our present status as holy ones
in Christ affects not only our present life but also our life in the age to
come.

The phrase "in Ephesus" which describes the saints is missing in
some important manuscripts, but as discussed in the introduction, a solid
case can be made for their original inclusion. An important caveat is that

Paul would have understood believers living in the outlying towns around Ephesus as recipients as well. Paul does something similar in 2 Cor 1:1 wherein he addresses not only the Corinthians but all who live throughout Achaia, for Corinth was the lead city in that region. I would add that in 1 Cor 1:2 Paul addresses the letter not only to the church in Corinth, but to believers everywhere. Parenthetically, this is interesting in as much as 1 Corinthians deals with very specific problems and questions generated by that local church. Paul presents his response as required reading for the whole church, not just the Corinthians. My point is that Paul can speak very specifically about local issues that he believes are pertinent to the entire church; this suggests that Paul can likewise speak generally to a wide audience. Thus when Paul wrote he was speaking to the local community and its struggles, but also with an eye, or at least frequent glances, to the wider church, its mission in and witness to the world.

PAUL'S EULOGY (1:3–14)

³Praise be to the God and Father of our Lord Jesus Christ, who has blessed us in the heavenly realms with every spiritual blessing in Christ. ⁴For he chose us in him before the creation of the world to be holy and blameless in his sight. In love ⁵he predestined us for adoption to sonship through Jesus Christ, in accordance with his pleasure and will—⁶to the praise of his glorious grace, which he has freely given us in the One he loves. ⁷In him we have redemption through his blood, the forgiveness of sins, in accordance with the riches of God's grace ⁸that he lavished on us. With all wisdom and understanding, ⁹he made known to us the mystery of his will according to his good pleasure, which he purposed in Christ, ¹⁰to be put into effect when the times reach their fulfillment—to bring unity to all things in heaven and on earth under Christ. ¹¹In him we were also chosen, having been predestined according to the plan of him who works out everything in conformity with the purpose of his will, ¹²in order that we, who were the first to put our hope in Christ, might be for the praise of his glory. ¹³And you also were included in Christ when you heard

the word of truth, the gospel of your salvation. When you believed, you were marked in him with a seal, the promised Holy Spirit, [14]who is a deposit guaranteeing our inheritance until the redemption of those who are God's possession—to the praise of his glory.

Paul's eulogy serves to inform even as it praises. Key ideas and terms that will surface throughout the letter are introduced here. Even more, the context for those key thoughts is created, and the grand narrative of salvation history is briefly sketched, with certain segments to be filled in later in greater depth. The importance of this narrative cannot be overestimated for those who believe the teachings of Ephesians are directed not just to first-century believers, but to the church today. Key concepts like predestination, forgiveness, sonship, or grace do not merely float on the surface, as though they can be plucked from the letter and given definitions as part of a formal schema. Rather, Paul sets these terms within God's overarching story, beginning with creation and the fall and even before time itself, as Paul reaches back before the foundation of the world for his starting point to narrate God's activities in his own time and place, the first century CE in the Roman Empire.

This story includes two groups of characters, the Jews and the Gentiles. This reality comes into sharp focus in chapter 2, but here in chapter 1 Paul only touches upon it with his explanation about "we" who were first in Christ and "you" (Gentiles in Ephesus) who heard the gospel and believed. He expresses a similar thought in Rom 1:16, that the gospel came to the Jew first and then to the Gentile. The grand narrative of God's redemptive work must include a discussion or recognition at least of God's work in and through Israel and its prophets and promises. For Paul it is not the distinction between Jews and Gentiles which captures his attention—such was common knowledge and general experience in his day. Rather, what seized his imagination was their unity through the gospel.

Along with the grand narrative providing the foundation for Paul's thought, it has been suggested that the earliest use of this epistle was a baptismal catechesis. Principal terms found in Jesus' baptism story (see Matt 3:13–15; Mark 1:9–11; Luke 3:21–22; John 1:29–34) are also found here, including "Son" (Ephesians has "sonship"), "good pleasure," "beloved," and "Spirit." Additionally, forgiveness of sins was tied with baptism. Certainly the message of Ephesians is solid teaching for any new believer; however, we do not know enough about the rituals of the earliest Christians to draw any firm conclusions. Moreover, Paul also uses similar language in Rom 8:4–30, including "sonship" and "Spirit" along with "adoption," "inheritance," and "predestination." Yet Rom 8:4–30 is not understood as a baptismal text. The ten verses that make up the eulogy introduce key terms, but also state God's posture or attitude toward his creation, including humans, namely that God desires his people for himself. We find that God blesses, graces, and wills all for the benefit of his people, those who heeded the gospel invitation. Not only is God's character as one who abounds in grace established in Paul's eulogy, but also the method of demonstrating that grace is repeatedly emphasized: in Christ. The blessings are ours in Christ, as is our forgiveness, inheritance, and sonship. The full picture of Christ's greatness is developed in the thanksgiving (1:15–23). Here the emphasis is on how God worked in Christ to accomplish his purpose, that is, to sum up all things in Christ, including a people that are to the praise of God's glory. Nor can this plan be fully implemented without the work of the Holy Spirit who seals those who are in Christ. The third member of the Trinity not only secures the promises of salvation those in Christ enjoy, but also enables believers to resist the evil forces that do battle against the faithful (6:12, 18).

Structure of 1:3–14

Verses 1:3–14 form a eulogy or blessing to God the Father, who has extended grace through his Son, the Lord Jesus Christ. Verse 3 announces that God is blessed, and vv. 4–10 explain further why such a claim is valid, while vv. 11–14 show how these claims impact believers directly. One way to march through this passage is to note how Paul describes God's actions by focusing on the verbs (usually participles). Paul declares that God chose us (1:4), blessed us (1:6), and lavished his grace upon us (1:8). God the Father made known to us (1:9) what he also purposed (1:10), namely that he was summing up or uniting all things in Christ (1:10). Through God's power and by his will, we were made an inheritance (1:11) and were predestined (1:11) to be those whose corporate life is to the praise of God's glory. Both those who first heard (1:12) and those who have more recently attended to and believed the gospel (1:12) now are sealed (1:13) in the Holy Spirit assuring redemption, again to God's glory.

As crucial as are the participles, the prepositions that introduce the numerous clauses help govern the meaning and set the cadence of thought and speech. Both warrant careful attention as Paul expounds on the purposes of God, demonstrated in his all-surpassing grace that manifests itself in the redemptive work of Christ. For example, the phrases "in Christ" and "in the Lord" occur frequently. Not to put too fine a point on it, but in general, Paul uses the term "Christ" when referring to the crucified and resurrected Messiah, and the term "Lord" in the context of discussing the functional aspects of a believer's life as they seek to live out the reality of their salvation. Paul also uses "in whom" (meaning Christ) in 1:7, 11, 13, highlighting three special privileges believers enjoy based on their relationship with Christ. The preposition "in" designates union rooted in the historical events of the cross and resurrection. The dative case used here gives the sense of "through" Christ, and also the sense of location, namely that believers are where Christ also is. Finally the dative denotes identity, such that just as Paul can speak of those who are "in Adam" or "in Abraham" so too believers are in Christ; we share a particular identity as a group in which each individual also bears this identity.

The section 1:4–6 forms a sub-unit of thought, explaining why it is that God could be so richly described in 1:3. Then 1:7–10 develops the mystery of Christ's redemption work, leading to 1:11–14, which explicates what that life in Christ is to the believer. Certain key terms and phrases connect these three units. For example, in 1:4, 12 the verb "to be" in the infinitive is used with similar purpose. In the former verse, God's choosing us in Christ was to make us holy and blameless. In the latter verse, God's will was that we be for the praise of his glory, the goal to which God's work in Christ (1:4) naturally leads. Additionally, Paul provides bridges of key terms or concepts between the sub-units to help guide the reader. For instance, in 1:4 he notes God's plan that believers are to be in Christ was established before the foundations of the world, and in 1:5 he writes similarly that God predestined us to be in Christ. The same verb translated "predestined" in 1:5 is used in the passive tense in 1:11, further emphasizing God's choice in creating a people holy and blameless. He uses words that carry the prefix *eu* which stresses blessings. As we noted above, 1:3 uses this word family three times, and in 1:5, 9 we find the phrase "according to his good pleasure." And propelling the argument along are his many prepositions, including the numerous occurrences of *eis*, which introduces a clause indicating intention. When Paul writes in

1:5 that God predestined us *to* sonship, he is explaining the goal of the predestined decision. Again, in 1:9b–10 Paul clarifies that God's purpose in Christ was to bring his plan to accomplishment, namely the uniting or summing up of all things in Christ.

Blessings (1:3)

Verse three is Paul's thesis statement, which sets up his argument in the remaining ten verses. Three times Paul uses the Greek noun or verb cognate for "blessing" (from which we get our English word "eulogy"): God is the blessed one; he is the one who blessed us with all spiritual blessings. The full character of the Truine God is hinted at in the passage as well, for Paul notes that these blessings come from the Lord Jesus Christ's God and Father. Moreover, these blessings are spiritual blessings, and this adjective is fleshed out in 1:13 when we read of the promised Holy Spirit marking believers as their seal and assurance of redemption. The spiritual blessings are from/of/pertaining to the Holy Spirit; we should avoid the modern assumption that spiritual is limited to the non-physical realm and personal piety of individuals. It is God the Father's work in God the Son, affirmed in God the Holy Spirit, which Paul sets out to demonstrate in the remaining ten verses. Declaring God as Father evoked in the ancient world ideas of belonging to a family, of authority within the family, and responsibilities to raise upright and virtuous children. Both Jewish and Gentile fathers were expected to provide for their children. Today, however, identifying God as Father has come under sharp criticism, for at least two reasons. In some cases, the inadequacies, if not downright criminal behavior, of some fathers towards their children has emptied the term of all goodness. In other cases, fatherhood has been understood to emphasize maleness over against femaleness. We must note that the point here is not to promote fatherhood over motherhood. Moreover, the characteristics of God the Father are not limited to males, nor does Paul make the point that God is male; indeed the characteristics include love, mercy, grace, care, and responsibility toward children, often characteristics we associate today with women. In 1:17 Paul speaks of the father of glory, with the adjective "glory" summing up all the attributes of the Father just discussed in the eulogy: redemption of a people to be to the praise of his glory. When Paul speaks of Christ and God (Father) in terms of the redemptive work of Christ, as in 1 Cor 3:23; 11:3; 15:28, there is in view the economic Trinity, which focuses on how God is redeeming creation. The economic Trinity stresses distinction (Jesus Christ emptied himself) for the purposes of redemption. The ontological Trinity is the union of the Three-in-One which has no distinction in essence; all three are co-equally God. This verse (1:3) introduces the phrase "in the heavenly realms," a phrase used only in Ephesians, but found six times, suggesting its importance. The term "heavenly" is used in 1 Cor 15.48 (see also Phil 2:10), which contrasts the earthly body and the heavenly body, the earthly man and the heavenly man. Paul continues that flesh and blood cannot inherit the kingdom, and Paul reveals the mystery that at the last trumpet sound, the dead will rise imperishable. These terms, inherit and mystery, are found as well in Ephesians, with a similar point made: we have redemption through his blood, an inheritance. In Ephesians, "heavenly" is in the dative with the preposition *en*, which carries a sense of location. Why does he stress the dative of location in Ephesians? One reason could be because he is speaking about the vastness of God's power and the reach of Christ's redemptive work—even over the powers in the heavenly realms (3:10; 6:12). He argues that Christ has attained the victory over all powers and forces, and this victory is demonstrated through the church and each believer's faithful stand in Christ. Such a claim would sound particularly audacious to the average Ephesian who had in their own city one of the seven wonders of the ancient world, the Temple of Artemis. They would also see the pageantry of the imperial cult, and reflect on the vastness of the Empire's power, and scratch their heads at statements such as Paul makes here. Ironically today, only a single column from Artemis' grand edifice stands as a solitary witness amidst a swamp-like setting, crowned with a stork's nest. And great temples to the emperors survive only as scattered pieces of marble and a few arches hinting at their former glory.

Chosen through Christ (1:4–6)

A closer look at 1:4–6 shows a tightly packaged argument that stresses God's blessing which was lavishly extended. The key noun is grace; it is God's grace that manifests his blessing, it is God's grace that is so prolifically bestowed. Paul explains that it was always God's plan to redeem his world through the Lord Jesus Christ; indeed it was God's good pleasure that informed his will. An astonishing number of parallels are found with Rom 8, including specific concepts such as predestination, sonship, and

Spirit. Moreover, the general topic and mood is similar: God has chosen and redeemed a people to himself in Christ, and this claim is assured through the Spirit of God. Paul speaks of our sonship in Christ (8:15, 23 [perhaps]; Gal 4:5).

It is important to keep this picture of the gracious God central, as some of the discussion surrounding terms such as "predestine" can give rise to images of capriciousness or cavalier flippancy in a modern reader's mind. Either God is presented as fickle, choosing willy-nilly whomever he wants and also choosing to damn the rest, or God is seen as choosing some because in some way, however hidden it may be, they deserved it more than the others. Of course we usually don't voice either of these claims in quite such bald language, but nonetheless their unsettling presence, like ants at a picnic, intrudes inconveniently.

At issue are two points. First is the relative freedom for humans to respond to God's call, especially at the time of salvation. Second, what is Paul focused upon—initial entrance into God's family, or the ultimate end result of salvation? Said another way, is Paul talking about how one is saved, or to what purpose one is saved? The key point is whether in using the term "predestined" Paul intends to speak about election, hence about getting saved, or about the final redemption, the result of salvation, not the beginning of it. If used in the latter sense, the term predestined does not reference election per se but outcome; the one called will end up a certain way, namely looking like Jesus, being counted as a co-heir. And of course both these issues are inextricably intertwined with a full-orbed view of salvation, including redemption, the Christian life, and the new heavens and new earth. Denominational battle lines have been drawn over the nuances of this argument, and this quick study of a few of the pertinent verses will certainly not settle the problem. Laying out the issue may help readers process the concern and fit the puzzle pieces together as they think best.

In our Ephesians text, we find Paul connecting the finite verb "he chose" with the participle "having predestined." Paul uses the term "predestined" in 1:5, 11 and elsewhere in Rom 8:29, 30 (the verb is also used in Acts 4:28 and 1 Cor 2:7, referring to objects, not humans). In general, two schools of thought surface concerning the term's interpretation. One school promotes the interpretation that God is choosing some people (and not others, by implication at least) for salvation. A second school argues that God calls to all, and some respond; the latter then receive the promised inheritance or sonship, and are destined to become in the image of the Son. The Greek text in Rom 8:28 allows for this latter possibility, in that it reads "according to purpose" (the pronoun "his" does not appear in the Greek in this verse), which means that God calls all, but not all respond. The point here might be that Paul is assuring the believers (the ones loving God in 8:28) that God in his foreknowledge knew who would choose him, and prepared their sonship. He predestined them to be conformed to the image of the Son—their goal is sure and their means to achieve it as well. In the context of Eph 1:5, 11, the flow of Paul's argument is to praise God for his work through Christ to make a holy and blameless people, ones predestined to sonship, for the praise of his glory (1:5–6), and this was accomplished by the blood of Christ, which results in the forgiveness of sins and the summing up of all things in Christ (1:7–10). In 1:11 he links "predestined" with the argument that God has planned for "us" (likely meaning believers generally) to be for God's praise and glory. When Paul uses "predestined" he connects it with inheritance; when he speaks of redemption, he argues the efficacy of Christ's blood for the forgiveness of sins. Without putting too fine a point on it, the evidence here leans towards seeing "predestined" as connected with God accomplishing his goal of making a people holy to himself, which includes but is not limited to the salvation or election of particular individuals. Paul speaks about God's character which manifests itself in actions that take the initiative with humans.[1] With his emphasis on choosing and predestining, Paul follows the pattern laid down in the Old Testament. The Law and the Prophets make clear that God elected Israel not for any particular intrinsic quality on their part, but based on God's good pleasure. God chose Abraham, Jacob, David, and a host of other figures to witness to and extend his work and his mercy. God also chose the people Israel to be his holy people. Peter likewise speaks of believers as a chosen people, and continues in describing them as a royal priesthood and a holy nation—language taken from core Jewish convictions about God's actions in bringing about a people of his Name (1 Pet 2:9). For the earliest Jewish believers in Jesus, then, the notion of chosenness had deep roots in God's revelation to ancient Israel. Paul explains God chose us for

---

1. Paul speaks of the Corinthian believers being chosen by God; here the emphasis is on God's choice of those who are unimpressive in the world's estimation. God acted in this manner so that his wisdom would be known and no person could boast before him (1 Cor 1:26–31).

a purpose, namely that we would be holy and blameless. Does Paul intend here a moral or a forensic meaning? While the term "holy ones" in 1:1 carries the latter meaning—the believers are holy in Christ (see also Col 1:22)—in 1:4 a strong case can be made that holiness and blamelessness are the character traits that Christians should exhibit, to God's glory. Paul stresses this to the Thessalonians (1 Thess 4:3, 8) in his call that they heed the will of God, which is their holiness (sanctification). Additionally, in Phil 2:15 Paul exhorts the Philippians to behavior that is blameless and pure, for in so doing they will shine like stars amidst the ink-black night, the corrupt evil age. Paul's sentiment is similar to Christ's words in the Sermon on the Mount (Matt 5:48) that his followers should be perfect even as his Father is perfect.

To what end this pursuit of the moral life? Paul cautions in his exhortations to the Ephesians to avoid sexual immorality, greediness, and corrupt language. He then warns that the impure and immoral person has no inheritance in the kingdom of Christ and God (5:5). One reason, then, to pursue the moral life is that it will match behavior fitting for life in God's kingdom. A second reason follows from the first: Paul repeatedly refers to the age to come when all things will be under Christ's dominion, and evil will be no more. Those who are in Christ have shed the clothing of the old age (4:22–24) and put on their new self, which is in Christ. A moral life testifies to the change, for one is no longer enslaved to the present evil age, but is freed to live the life purposed by the loving God. None of these good deeds tips the heavenly scales (if there is such a thing!), but Paul's point is that something real does happen when the Spirit lives within a believer. That change from darkness to light should be evident in choices made for holiness and love. The new creation inaugurated by Christ's death and resurrection signals the ultimate fall of the present age, as well as each believer's new life, and the church's existence as witness to the new thing God is doing in his plan to bring to completion the new heavens and new earth.

Finally, the question of why moral behavior is important is answered in Paul's vision of the church as the temple of the Lord. Not only are individual believers called to live holy lives, but as God's people, the church is being built as the dwelling of God's Spirit (2:19–22). The call to moral goodness in Christ, then, is not simply an add-on option for the Christian, although frequently believers have trouble explaining why their deeds matter. But that is often because they lack a comprehensive understanding of salvation. Christ's redemption does not simply save our sorry little souls—it is so much bigger than that puny picture. Life in Christ means being a member of Christ's body, being shaped together into the temple wherein the Holy Spirit dwells, and in the unity of that Spirit accomplishing the work of God prepared by God for his people to do. Both Jews and Gentiles knew all about temples, these were sacred spaces marked out by and for the deity. They were somewhat intimidating places, inasmuch as the deity was seen to be active there. Thus all people took great care to be pure or acceptable before entering the sacred space (obviously this looked different depending on whether you were a Jew or a Gentile). Christians, unlike the pagans and the Jews, did not have a sacred space, although the Jerusalem temple continued to be revered by Jewish Christians. Instead (more about this follows in the next chapter), Paul declares that believers themselves make up God's temple. Because that is the case, the ancient believer would track well with Paul's claim that, as a stone in God's temple, I must be holy in my actions. To do otherwise would desecrate a holy site—a terrible, unthinkable offense.

At the end of 1:4 we have the clause "in love," but its referent is debated. Does it modify the previous clause "holy and blameless" or the following participle "predestined"? Arguments from grammar end in a draw, and one is left with determining the answer from the context. While it is without doubt that Paul believes all our actions should be covered with love, in this specific argument it is not believers who are the primary focus, but God. Additionally, at the end of 1:6, when Paul wraps up this particular thought, we find Paul describing Christ as the Beloved. This is the only place Paul describes Jesus in these terms (for a similar term, see Col 1:13), however, the Synoptic Gospels use it in describing Jesus' baptism and transfiguration (Matt 3:17, 17:5; Mark 1:11, 9:7; Luke 3:22; 9:35). It would be in keeping with Paul's rhetorical flourish that he would begin and end this thought with a similar term, love. Therefore, the balance of evidence tips in favor of understanding "in love" in connection with "predestined." Paul is asserting that God predestined out of his love.

Redemption in Christ (1:7–10)

Paul describes Christ the Beloved as the one in whom believers have redemption, specifically the forgiveness of transgressions through his shed blood. Paul does not seek to prove the validity of his statement. There is no hint that he is defending the necessity of the Christ's cross, as to the Corinthians. The truth that God has redeemed us through the blood of Christ appears to be a common assessment between Paul and his readers. More difficult to determine is whether Paul understands redemption to include in this case the idea of payment of ransom. Generally the term means deliverance, but it can include the sense of paying for release. If ransom is implicit, then the verse would be interpreted as Christ's death being a ransom for our transgressions.

In this section Paul introduces a key term, "mystery." In Ephesians this term is tightly tied with the notion of unity in Christ. In 1:10 the unity is cosmic, namely that both heavenly and earthly things will finally be united in Christ at the end. But some measure of this mystery has already been put into effect, namely the unity within the church, the one-ness in Christ of Jew and Gentile in God's plan to make a people unto himself (3:5). It has been claimed that Paul describes mystery with a different nuance in 1 Cor 15:51, and that therefore its use here suggests a deutero-Pauline author. But two points should be noted. First, "mystery" as a concept allows for some fluidity; it is not a rigid category in Paul's time. Second, that said, in both 1 Corinthians and Ephesians, the general context of "mystery" is similar. In 1 Cor 15:56 Paul notes that the power of sin is the law—and yet he had not been speaking about Jews and Gentiles in this chapter, or to any extent throughout the letters, so why note it here? Because the law served to separate Gentiles from Jews, while Christ brought the two groups together, through faith. The mystery, for Paul, is the marvelous act of mercy that redeemed both Jew and Gentile, and created for God one unified people (2:15). Additionally, this mystery is now *revealed*, not hidden. Paul's understanding of "mystery" has little resemblance in this sense, then, to the mystery cults that dotted the Roman religious landscape.[2] Rome was both suspicious and sometimes tolerant of these private groups with their closely guarded initiation rites that promised life after death, based on the dying-and-rising savior figure of their god or goddess. The Isis cult was especially popular, and a marvelously entertaining work from antiquity describing it has survived: *The Golden Ass* or *The Metamorphoses* by Apuleius. Josephus, the Jewish historian of the late first century CE, recounts a fascinating tale of a wealthy Roman

---

2. For a lengthy discussion on "mystery," see the chapter on Eph 3.

matron who was a member of the Isis cult.[3] A peer who was infatuated with her tricked her into having sex with him by posing as Isis' consort. He was exiled from Rome, his accomplice, a freedwoman, was crucified, and the matron's honor was restored. Of course, we cannot say whether this story was historical, but Josephus thinks it is, which indicates for our purposes that in the imagination of the ancients, the mystery cults were a significant part of the religious landscape. It is difficult to know how many participated in these mystery cults, but devotees came from across the social spectrum. Christian groups might at first glance appear as a mystery cult, but that impression would not bear up under scrutiny. Paul notes the mystery of God is revealed. The mystery is accomplished in full view, and no initiation money is required to join.

Fusing the Horizons: God's Plan, Uniting All Things in Christ

Paul hints in 1:10 of the enormity of God's plan in his statement that all things will be united in Christ, both in heaven and on earth. N. T. Wright has said that "we must envisage a world in which the present creation, which we think of in those three dimensions [space, time and matter], is enhanced, taken up into God's larger purposes, no doubt, but certainly not abandoned."[4] The resurrection of Jesus indicates that God did not reject his creation, but seeks to redeem it through Christ. Our worship and our mission should be eschatologically focused. That means we do away with the dualism between spirit and body, which in church missions looked like saving souls without tending to bodily needs. Instead, a humble church should sing notes of grace to the present world. God's redemptive work establishing the church as a beachhead in this present age means that believers should engage in bringing God's mercy, justice, and grace to our communities at all levels—schools, hospitals, and governments—as a real, natural, and expected part of the church's conviction that Christ is now Lord of all, not just of believers' hearts. The homeless shelters, arts in the community programs, financial help for disadvantaged, and so much more are the concrete expressions of the conviction that God in Christ has redeemed the world, and that Christ is Lord *now* over all

3. Josephus *Ant.* 18.65–80.
4. Wright 2008: 259.

creation. Believers have the right and responsibility to stand fast against the human injustices that wreak havoc on so many individuals and communities, and also to stand firm against the spiritual forces at work behind the scenes fomenting injustice, disobedience to God, and just plain evil (Eph 6:12). As the church lives out the resurrection truth, not only will bullies and crooks seek to push the church back into its building with instructions to pay attention to its own business (understood as saving souls), but the church will also face spiritual forces that rail against God's goodness and grace extended to his earthly creation. In the former case, Paul calls on believers to live out of their new self and be holy, imitate God (5:1). In the latter case, Paul declares that the church's very existence challenges the powers and principalities (3:10), and so the church must stand firm in God's armor against the onslaught of evil's final frantic bid for power (6:13).

Sealed with the Spirit (1:11–14)

Paul discusses in closer detail the redemptive act of God in Christ, and more fully discusses the Christian's gain in Christ. Specifically, in Christ believers are part of the predestined plan of God to bring him praise through Christ. Paul describes believers as "we" and "you," distinguishing those who first were in Christ and those who became members of the family later. This division is more sharply defined in the following chapter in terms of Jew and Gentile, and here, although the terms are not used, it seems likely that at least a key distinguishing characteristic of the two groups is their Jewish or non-Jewish status. The third Person of the Trinity, the Holy Spirit, is spotlighted as the believer's seal of assurance for redemption, looking ahead to the eschatological age. Once again we find Paul using the terms "predestined" and "appointed" (sometimes translated as "made" or "obtain an inheritance"). The latter verb (aorist passive) is found only here in the New Testament. In the wider Greek world the verb is connected with casting lots to appoint a position (as the disciples do in Acts 1:26) and by extension, inheritance. The passive voice can support the interpretation that God has made believers his inheritance. And this would fit with the upcoming claim that God's plan is to make a people that are to the praise of his glory (1:12). But the verb can also be interpreted as believers being appointed an inheritance by

God. This interpretation finds support in Col 1:12, where the cognate noun is used in the phrase "to share in the inheritance of his people in the kingdom of light." If the latter interpretation is followed, we have Paul explaining that the believers' inheritance is established (predestined) by God's plan in Christ. Paul underscores the aspect of God's predestined plan to counter any hints that the appointment by lot was arbitrary from God's perspective. However, the verb is useful in its association with casting lots inasmuch as this reflects Paul's insistence that humans cannot win through merit God's gracious salvation. So from a human perspective, God's choice is not based on the world's judgment of what is good (as Paul indicates to the Corinthians in 1 Cor 1:26, not many of them were wise or outstanding from a social standpoint). But from God's perspective, the choice always had his full will and wish behind it. Further support for this reading is Paul's description of the believer's inheritance as assured by the promised Holy Spirit which seals each member of Christ's body (1:14).

Fusing the Horizons: Election, Predestination, and Free Will

As noted above, much effort and debate has centered on the important questions of election, predestination, and human free will. Each age has entertained a particular focus, from as far back as Origen's debate with the Gnostics, and Augustine's argument with Pelagius. As each person and church fellowship works through these crucial questions, I would offer a few points to keep in mind. First, and probably most important, as we will see in Eph 3–6 (over half of the letter), Paul insists that Christians live a moral life—and not just because it is more pleasant to be around a moral person. Indeed Paul claims that each believer is now a new person, clothed with Christ, a "new man" (or woman) who must mature in Christ (4:13). Any claims of human free will and God's sovereignty should make space for the real-time (present) necessity of holy living. Second, and closely related to the first, Paul does not place such emphasis on the individual as to relegate the corporate body secondary status. For Paul, there is no isolated believer—all can only function in community. Any discussion of election must include appreciation for both individual and corporate membership in God's salvation plan. Third, down through the centuries it has been tempting to see election and predestination through dualistic lens, whereby an individual's soul is elected and it floats to heaven at death.

But Paul's vision of the new age to come is rooted firmly on the renewed terra firma. Our salvation will be lived out in a resurrected body on a renewed earth. Any discussion of free will and election should have a robust vision of the totality of God's salvation "package." Finally, I confess that I enjoy Paul's agility to move between absolute conviction in God's unstoppable plan, determined by his will and pleasure alone, and humankind's accountability, based on choice, to be responsible for their actions as they relate to God's plan of salvation. It is a posture worth emulating, for it promotes humility as believers search the deep truth of God.

A further point bears pondering. Often in the debate about God's sovereignty and human free will, Western white readers struggle with and are suspicious of the ramifications of God's absolute power. In Western democracies, citizens have grown accustomed to using their voice at the ballot box to effect change or keep the status quo. However, the earliest believers for the most part were poor, often marginalized, even slaves. Few had citizenship (either Roman or within their city). Few were wealthy, and many were persecuted. Given this backdrop, the promise of a God who has authority over all powers and authorities—and even more that this God has chosen them—reorients their understanding of reality. Though for the moment they might be beaten or denied justice or languish from lack of food or medical care (such as it was), in the reality that really matters, they were chosen by the God of the universe. A modern example might help. I lived in Kenya for three years as an American citizen abroad. If trouble occurred or if natural disaster were to strike, I could escape the consequences by using my U.S. passport backed by the strength and reputation of the United States government. So too, Paul declares that both the earliest Christians and believers today have such a passport: the seal of the Spirit, which guarantees not their present personal well-being, but their ultimate, eternal safety. God is for them—they have nothing to fear (see Rom 8:31).

In 1:11, Paul notes that in Christ believers enjoy an inheritance. In 1:13 we find a similar phrase "in him" used twice, with aorist participles, indicating that the two clauses work together with the third main verb "you were sealed." This means that at the moment one hears and believes, one is sealed with the Holy Spirit. Paul also speaks to the Ephesian believers ("you") as those who heard the message of truth after he and those with him ("we") heard the good news. The contrast between them is based on when a person heard the good news, but the chronological distinction hints as well to the salvation pattern enacted by God to the Jew first and then to the Gentile (Rom 1:16). All are saved alike, but not all are the same before being in Christ. Jews had the advantages of God's self-revelation in the Law and worship at the temple. Jews were monotheists; Gentiles were polytheists, pantheists, or panentheists. Paul will expand on this in the next chapter. Here we should hear Paul's emphasis that God's promise in Christ is for all, Jew and Gentile. The proof, if you will, is in the Spirit. For the early church, second only to the amazing truth of Christ's resurrection was the reality of the Spirit indwelling all believers—including Gentiles. This is Peter's great discovery in Acts 10:1—11:18, that God shows no favoritism, inasmuch as Gentiles, as Gentile believers, receive the Holy Spirit. So too Paul declares in Eph 1:14 that the Holy Spirit is a seal or surety of a believer's inheritance, namely the redemption of those who are saved in Christ to God's glory. The Holy Spirit of promise points to the eschatological future. In 1:3 Paul states believers have been blessed with every spiritual blessing, and here we find the Spirit of promise, implying things to come, and also the seal of the Spirit who is active now. The grand sweep of God's loving salvation story as willed and accomplished by the Father, Christ, and the Holy Spirit—past, present, and future—stretches our imagination.

PAUL'S PRAYER (1:15–23)

> [15]For this reason, ever since I heard about your faith in the Lord Jesus and your love for all his people, [16]I have not stopped giving thanks for you, remembering you in my prayers. [17]I keep asking that the God of our Lord Jesus Christ, the glorious Father, may give you the Spirit of wisdom and revelation, so that you may know him better. [18]I pray that the eyes of your heart may be enlightened in order that you may know the hope to which he has called you, the riches of his glorious inheritance in his people, [19]and his incomparably great power for us who believe. That power is the same as the mighty strength [20]he exerted when he raised Christ from the dead and seated him at his right hand in the heavenly realms,

²¹far above all rule and authority, power and dominion, and every name that can be invoked, not only in the present age but also in the one to come. ²²And God placed all things under his feet and appointed him to be head over everything for the church, ²³which is his body, the fullness of him who fills everything in every way.

This last section of chapter 1 recounts Paul's prayer, one rich in theological nuance. Several points should be noted, not the least of which is that this prayer is grounded in the attitude of thanksgiving. The content of his prayer includes three key components: that the believers would know (1) the hope of their calling, (2) the wealth of their inheritance, and (3) the mighty power of God which raised Jesus from the dead. Paul offers this prayer not for individual believers as though they can fully attain this on their own, but imagines this prayer being fulfilled or accomplished in community. These are not private goals, in other words, but community goals, the pursuit of which must happen in the church. I might note here parenthetically that those who claim Ephesians only imagines the church universal fail to appreciate that Paul prays God will accomplish his will in each believer's life as they experience life in the community of the faithful. Though it is true that the church universal is Christ's body, it is equally true that Paul imagines believers will experience the inheritance of God in their local community, where their gifts are exercised and their good works are realized by God's power.

When Paul prays for them, he never fails to thank God for them. This attitude is based on their faith in Christ and their expressions of love to the saints. It is too easy to fall into the trap so eloquently observed by G. K. Chesterton, namely, loving humanity but hating people. Paul does not simply thank God in some esoteric sense or with superficial awareness of the Ephesians' situation. He declares that their walk with God has produced actual results in the form of loving acts on behalf of their brothers and sisters in the Lord. One is reminded of John's comments that people cannot declare their love of God, while at the same time harboring deep resentment or anger towards God's children. Paul is proud of the Ephesians, he is happy that they have demonstrated a working faith, a sincere commitment to the community of faith. Indeed, these words of thanks are not idle or shallow, but based on actual postures of obedience within the Ephesian community. The basis of growth in the Christian life is to understand who God is and who we are in Christ. Thus Paul asks first that God will grant a spirit of wisdom and revelation that opens believers' awareness to the great things of God. We know God because God chooses to reveal himself. In 1:18, we find a participial phrase stating that the eyes of their hearts have been enlightened. This phrase can be understood in two ways, either as part of Paul's request or as a statement of the Ephesians' current condition in Christ. The latter option is better in as much as it takes into account the tense (perfect passive), and connects the "you" in 1:17 with the "you" in 1:18 by reminding them that they have already been equipped and prepared to receive God's wisdom because their hearts were flooded with God's light. As believers, Paul notes that already our hearts have been enlightened, so that God is able to further lead us in the discovery of his greatness.

Paul includes three requests: that they might know the hope of their calling, might appreciate their inheritance, and might recognize the power that makes the first two a reality. Paul will expand upon the idea of calling at the beginning of ch. 4, but we can note here that his calling offers future promise. We are called but have yet to achieve all that is part of that calling; hence we assume a posture of hope. Likewise, Paul asks that our knowledge of God be further developed in light of his inheritance in the saints. The possessive pronoun gives pause here: Is Paul stating that God's own inheritance is that he has saints in Christ? Or is the genitive indicating that God's inheritance is given to the saints? In favor of the latter is 1:14, which notes that the Spirit is our seal, securing our inheritance in Christ. But 1:11 states that believers are God's inheritance in Christ, and 1:18 might be continuing that thought, namely that the saints would have their minds opened to the amazing truth that the church is God's possession. Finally, Paul asks that God would reveal his tremendous power, which not only raised Christ from the dead, but works also on our behalf as believers. Before we examine more closely Paul's description of God's power in Christ's resurrection and the tectonic shift in spiritual powers that ensued, we might pause to reflect on the characterization of believers thus far. The saints have faith in Christ and love for the saints. Their faith in the Lord Jesus is not simply a nod to God's activity in Christ's death and resurrection. The events create a community of faith, a community distinguished by love. Even as in 1:4 the believers are chosen to be holy and blameless in love, later in ch. 1 their actions are covered by, energized by, understood through love. Also, God intends that his inheritance is a people for the praise of his glory. Believers are those who live in hope; here is Paul's eschatology peaking through. Believers are to live in God's power, which encompasses Christ's death, the forgiveness of sins, and the resurrection. The great power that raised the dead Jesus will also raise each believer; this is our inheritance. The power is greater than any imaginable, for it takes account of this world and the next.

In the last three verses of ch. 1, Paul reflects on the greatness of Christ in several ways. First, he notes that Christ is seated at God's right hand, the place of special commendation in the ancient world (Ps 110:1). Second, Paul notes that Christ's place is above every spiritual power, in this world and the world to come. This must be the case, otherwise our resurrection cannot be assured, for the possibility might exist that in the age to come, Christ's power would be insufficient against the spiritual forces. Paul assures believers that the future will hold no surprises. The subordination of all powers has occurred; they are under his feet, and he is their head. Third, Christ is head over all things "to the church," which is in the dative. The sense here is difficult to determine. It may be a dative of advantage, which would mean that Christ is head "for the church." But the dative could indicate indirect object, which would indicate that God gave Christ as head to the church. The dative might be a dative of instrument, that God appointed Christ as head so that he could rule all things through the church. Fourth, the church is described as Christ's body, an image Paul will continue to develop in the epistle. Finally, the final clause describes the fullness of the one filling all in all. Does this "fullness" refer to the church or Christ? If the former, then the church is the receptacle of Christ's fullness, and also continues to be filled by God. In this interpretation, believers represent Christ not simply as forgiven sinners, but as containing within the church the fullness of God's plan of redemption, the first scent of hope and promise to a world decaying in sin. The church is integral to God's plan in Christ to make known to the powers now and in the age to come His greatness and glory. If, however, we see "fullness" referring to Christ, the accent is on Christ completely filling all things. In this reading, Christ's body can be characterized as representing his fullness. The former reading makes better sense of the latter terms in the clause, namely that God is the one who fills all in all. Although it is a difficult passage to interpret, the most likely reading of

1:23 is that Paul describes the church, Christ's body, as Christ's fullness. And Christ's fullness is from God the Father, who is all in all (see 1 Cor 15:28, Col 1:19; 2:9).

EPHESIANS 2

With the exception of John 3:16, perhaps the most famous passage in Scripture is "by grace you have been saved, through faith," found in Eph 2:8 (see also 2:6). The challenge is to hear this verse anew, to have it speak afresh. With that goal in mind, let us imagine ourselves as part of an early second-century Christian church in a little town about fifteen miles from Ephesus, a small community of perhaps a dozen or so like-minded Gentiles. We heard the gospel from a traveling missionary, and had a copy of Ephesians as our main guide to the Christian life. Paul's letters to the Romans, the Corinthians, the Philippians and the Thessalonians were unknown to our tiny group. What would our Christian life look like, what would be its major contours and emphases?

As we have seen, the resounding note that rings loudly in the opening chapter of the epistle, which reverberates and echoes in the remaining chapters, is God's amazing plan of sonship for his people through Christ as part of an overarching design to redeem and renew creation. Chapter 2 picks up the melody line, and adds accompaniment, filling out the purposes of God for the church. I think our second-century community would expect that the gospel gives new hope by granting membership into a special group—the people of God. Salvation by faith was viewed as having two dimensions to it, equally important and explaining each other. Salvation in Christ took our little group from the kingdom of darkness to the kingdom of light by giving each of us new life in Christ. This new life in the new kingdom was actually a new humanity, realized in Christ through the Spirit by faith. Salvation was understood by these early believers not only in individualistic terms, nor as merely a private decision, nor as something that affected only the human soul. Paul instructs all believers that salvation brings us into God's family, it makes us part of his holy temple, and its blessings usher us into the next, new age.

RAISED WITH CHRIST (2:1–10)

¹As for you, you were dead in your transgressions and sins, ²in which you used to live when you followed the ways of this world and of the ruler of the kingdom of the air, the spirit who is now at work in those who are disobedient. ³All of us also lived among them at one time, gratifying the cravings of our sinful nature and following its desires and thoughts. Like the rest, we were by nature deserving of wrath. ⁴But because of his great love for us, God, who is rich in mercy, ⁵made us alive with Christ even when we were dead in transgressions— it is by grace you have been saved. ⁶And God raised us up with Christ and seated us with him in the heavenly realms in Christ Jesus, ⁷in order that in the coming ages he might show the incomparable riches of his grace, expressed in his kindness to us in Christ Jesus. ⁸For it is by grace you have been saved, through faith—and this is not from yourselves, it is the gift of God—⁹not by works, so that no one can boast. ¹⁰For we are God's handiwork, created in Christ Jesus to do good works, which God prepared in advance for us to do.

These ten verses contain crucial theological truth, ethical challenge, and exegetical puzzles. To understand the former two, we need to pay attention to the latter. One central question affecting the reading is Paul's use of the pronouns "you" and "we." If we attend carefully to these pronouns, the depth of Paul's argument will become clearer.

You and *We* in Paul's Argument

Who are the "you" in Paul's argument? While of course the scripture speaks to each of us, and we can all place ourselves in the shoes of the "you" who are dead in trespasses and sins (2:1), Paul has in mind here not the generic human, but the Gentile. It is the Gentile who lived as part of this present age, ruled by evil forces and sinful attitudes. This age is dominated by abuse of power, greed, hatred—summed up as disobedience against God. In 2:3 Paul shifts his gaze from Gentile to Jew, and notes that "we" Jews are not innocent of wrongdoing, because we operated under the influence of the flesh. A similar toggle between "you" and "we" is found in Col 2:11–14. Paul notes that the Gentile believers were (spiritually) circumcised in Christ, paralleling this image with that of their baptism. He continues that their uncircumcised nature was made alive in Christ. But then Paul speaks of Christ's forgiveness, and here he uses "we" to celebrate the canceled debt that had condemned all humans. Paul's message in Rom 7:5 is relevant here: the flesh (sinful nature) works against the good law of God, causing Jews who love the law to disobey it. Jews and Gentiles are equally guilty before God, but they arrive at their guilty status from different paths. Gentiles are idolaters; they have forsaken the one true God and follow idols. Jews know God's revelation, and have the advantages of the Law, the prophets, the temple, the promises, the covenants (see Rom 9:4–5), but they have not all acted from the wellspring of faith. So in the end, all are in need of God's grace.

Why is it important to emphasize this difference between Jews and Gentiles? First, because it is the best way to make sense of Paul's later argument that Christ's power is seen in making the two groups into one people. Paul believes that the two becoming one body is a powerful mystery, mysterious because it is so grand, so bold a plan, and powerful because through this one body, the church, God is declaring to the rulers and the authorities his unsearchable grace and unfathomable love. The miraculous creation of a new people, holy and wholly devoted to God, stands against the claims of the present age. The world calls for domination, selfishness, and independence from others and God, but God's grace given without respect of person (to Jew, Gentile, free, slave, male, female, and any other division humanity can think up) decisively ends all conversation (3:10). In and with Christ, the church, the two being one, stands as a testimony to God's love and power over against the social and political divisions that characterize our world. In a similar vein, Paul declares to the Philippians that by standing in one spirit for the faith of the gospel, they prove their opponents' destruction, and the Philippians' own salvation (Phil 1:27–28).

Second, focusing on the use of "you" and "we" helps explain why Paul declares "you have been saved" in 2:6, 8, rather than "we have been saved." Note that in 2:4 Paul introduces the subject of this long sentence (the sentence in Greek runs nine verses), namely God, and in 2:5–6 we have the main verbs: made alive, raised, and seated. Each of these verbs is in the past tense (aorist), indicating that God has done and finished with the deed. We will return to look more closely at the meanings of these verbs below, but here I want to note that Paul includes himself and all Jewish believers ("we") together with the Gentile believers ("you") in these acts of God. But in the middle of this great claim, he switches to using the second-person plural—"by grace you have been saved" (2:6). Why not say "*we* have been saved"? I think the verb tense is important. The verb is in the perfect tense, both here and in 2:8, which indicates that a past action has continuing relevance at the present. Unlike the other three verbs, which indicate a past action finished and done with, this verb indicates a continuing activity. That is why some translate the verb as "you are saved" rather than "you have been saved." The verb carries both meanings. An analogy might help. I am married; that is my current state, but it implies a past starting point, my wedding. The effect of the wedding is that I am currently and have been married. The power of my vows and my husband's vows remain in effect. So too God's promises in Christ remain effective against sin. Thus the present state owes itself to a past action by God in Christ, but that past action is not the whole story. The action is an ongoing one, you were saved and are saved—salvation has a beginning, middle, and end.

Salvation for Paul is not a ticket into heaven for your soul, but the entrance into fellowship with God and his people. As such, Paul is assuring the Gentiles that *you* are part of that salvation plan, *you* are now a citizen of God's kingdom, *you* are part of God's new temple. In Paul's day, Jews who believed in Christ would have already appreciated that they were part of God's family, and they would have understood the community aspect of God working through his people to reveal his love and mercy to the world. But for Gentiles, this was a staggering, astounding concept. Therefore twice Paul states it, so the readers would be clear: *you* Gentiles are saved by grace; all the promises, hopes, power, and responsibilities of citizenship in God's kingdom have been advanced to you in Christ.

One further pronoun shift should be noted, the shift from "you" in 2:1, referring to those "being dead in transgressions," to "we" in 2:5, "being those dead in transgressions." The same Greek participle and nouns are used, only the pronoun varies. At first glance it might appear that Paul in these verses is generalizing all humanity into believer and non-believer categories. However, in 2:1 those being dead in trespasses are further explained as walking in the ways of this world and following the ways of this present age. Jews have God's revelation, so they can discern truth from falsehood (idols). But because both Jews and Gentiles ultimately sin by either following the gods of this world or their own fleshly desires, the end result is that all are in need of God's grace. The transgressions might look different, one pursuing idolatry, another lusts of the flesh, but both paths take one far from the center of God's love. That is why Paul can also say that both *we* (Jews) and all the rest of humanity were children of wrath by nature (2:3). The emphasis is not on how each group came to such a situation (original sin discussion) or on whether people have been created for wrath (double predestination discussion). Rather, Paul's focus is on what state humanity is in at the present: they are under the power of sin and death.

Verb Tenses in Paul's Argument

Returning to the main verbs in 2:5–6, Paul describes God's actions towards believers who were once dead in trespasses as having made them alive with Christ, raised them with Christ, and seated them with Christ. Paul uses the past tense (aorist), which some suggest speaks against Pauline authorship. They argue that Paul focused on the future hope we have in Christ. The point Paul makes here, however, is that believers are *with* Christ, and so if they are with him, then they will share his current status and situation. Since Christ was indeed raised from the dead, if we are then *with* him, we share that resurrection status (see Col 2:12; 3:1). The reality of the resurrection life does not begin at Christ's second coming, it is occurring right now. Often in Pauline studies this eschatology is identified as a "now, not yet" position. *Now* in Christ we have all we need for living a holy life in the power of the Spirit, but *yet to come* is the resurrected body and new heavens and earth. And over all this is the reality that because we are in Christ, we share with Christ all the blessings of God through Christ. Such language is found in Rom 6:8, where Paul uses the future tense to speak about our hope in Christ, and past tense in Rom 8:30 to describe our standing in Christ as predestined, called, justified, and glorified.

Salvation Is God's Gift

Paul insists that God's grace is what provides salvation. In 2:8 he continues his claim in 2:5, "by grace you have been saved," with the additional clause "through faith." He follows with the qualifier "and this is not from yourselves, it is the gift of God." Several questions rise to the surface, including the meaning of "through faith" as well as the antecedent of "this" and the meaning of "gift." To the first point, many understand "through faith" to be the individual's subjective appropriation of God's salvation. Paul's point is that God's salvation is accepted on the basis of trust and confidence in God's promises and deeds worked in Christ Jesus that make possible salvation (Gal 2:16). However, some point to Phil 3:9 as a parallel ("through faith in/of Christ") and argue that the genitive construction "faith in/of Christ" is best understood as the "faithfulness of Christ." In Eph 2:8, they argue that Paul's meaning is best conveyed as "you have been saved through the faithfulness of Christ."[1] The latter position has the advantage of reinforcing Paul's overall point that it is God who saves; human effort is not part of the equation. Weakening this interpretation, however, is the fact that the genitive phrase "of/in Christ" is not found in Ephesians. To the second point, Paul speaks of "this" which is not of ourselves. To what is he referring? "This" is a neuter word, while both "faith" and "grace" are feminine. It is not grammatically impossible that "this" refers back to either of these words. The immediately previous noun "faith" is often pointed to as the antecedent; Paul thus is saying that faith itself is God's gift. However, this is not the most natural reading of the grammar. Some point to the verb participle "you have been saved," as the reference, but this participle is masculine, which again makes it less likely the antecedent. Most probably, "this" refers back to the entire argument Paul has made in the last few verses, namely, that one's salvation is God's gracious act done from and through his abundant love and mercy.

The third feature of this passage to be highlighted is Paul's term "gift." The word used here for "gift" (*dōron*) is not found elsewhere in Paul, although it was a common term in his day. The word is used by other New Testament writers often in the context of offering sacrifices (Matt 5:23–4; 23:18–19; Heb 5:1; 8:3–4). A related term (*dōrea*) is used in Eph 3:7; 4:7 (see also Rom 3:24; 5:15, 17; 2 Cor 9:15) and has the sense of an unmerited or undeserved gift or benefit. A third word for gift, *charisma*, is related to the word for "grace" (*charis*). *Charisma* is frequently used when speaking of the spiritual gifts of the Holy Spirit (Rom 12:6; 1 Cor 12:4) or a gift of office through the laying on of hands (1 Tim 4:14). We cannot

---

1. For a brief discussion of the options, see O'Brien 1999: 175.

know conclusively why Paul used *dōron* in Eph 2:8; however, its closeness to *dōrea*, used by Paul to express the extreme generosity of God's salvation, suggests this was Paul's intention as well in 2:8.

Grace through Faith, Not Works

Paul stresses that salvation is by grace, through faith, not works. If the analysis above is accurate, then at this point Paul is especially focused on the Gentiles' salvation in Christ. So why would Paul contrast grace and works? Typically the term "works" is understood as deeds done to earn merit before God. Would a Gentile be thinking like this? Paul cautions the Corinthians that God's choice of the foolish and weak was to prevent anyone from boasting before him (1 Cor 1:28, see also 4:7). And in Rom 2:1–16 a strong case can be made that Paul is talking about Gentiles (he first mentions Jews specifically in 2:17). If so, then Gentiles appeared to be tempted to focus on deeds; Paul speaks of those deeds done with evil intent being condemned by God. Gentiles have not earned God's approval, any more than Jews earn God's approval. Paul cautioned the Roman Gentile believers not to be haughty over against Jews (Rom 11:18), and the same attitude might be in view here. Ethnic pride and identity ran quite deep in the ancient world, and Paul addresses it head-on as it presented a grave danger to the church's unity. There is no place for boasting in oneself in the church.

Quite the opposite of boasting, grace has been a central theme from the beginning of the epistle, emphasized in 1:6–7 in connection with God's glory and his generosity. Grace is that favor which is unmerited, undeserved, and even unexpected (from a human standpoint). The muscular arm of God reaching to Adam as painted by Michelangelo on the Sistine chapel's ceiling calls to mind the grace of God inasmuch as God's grace is active, not static or theoretical. God's grace calls, saves, brings life. God's grace pursues those who are running from him (Rom 5:8). God's grace is grounded in and grows from his bottomless love, as Paul stresses in 2:4. In sum, Paul argues that believers are saved in Christ on the basis of grace.

Interestingly, Paul does not use the term "justified" here, but rather "saved." Ephesians is unique in Paul's letters in using the verb "saved" in the perfect tense in this context. Should we treat the terms as synonyms? Like level 5 river rapids, current discussions about the full import of

Paul's message of justification are treacherous waters to navigate, and participants tend to get very wet in the process. But the thrill of exploring the challenging waters of Paul's theology should encourage us to strap on the life jacket and grab an oar. I suggest that Paul uses "saved" here rather than "justified" because the latter term is too restrictive for his meaning. Said another way, I think Paul has already in so many words conveyed the concept of justification when he declared that we were made alive with Christ. God paved the way for new life by rescuing believers from their life of death, in Christ. This is the beginning of salvation, but it is not its sum total. New life today and resurrection life to come are a believer's secure fortune. In Rom 5:9–10, Paul speaks about justification and salvation, noting that the first makes way for the second. Justification comes through Christ's blood, it establishes the forgiveness of sins (see also Eph 1:7); that affects believers such that salvation from God's wrath is sure. Moreover, justification leads to reconciliation with God in the present. In Ephesians, by using the perfect tense, Paul suggests that the present enjoyment of God's salvation and the future assurance of deliverance from judgment are the benefits of each believer. Both Romans and Ephesians reassure the believer that God's covenant promises in Christ, in his death and resurrection, are firm and solid today, and will be on the last day.

Paul describes God's love and grace extended to believers in terms of being made alive with, raised with, and seated with Christ. With such benefits bestowed, a believer might begin to feel pretty special—all this attention, just for me? Paul nips such thoughts in the bud in 2:7. He notes that God has shown his great love and immeasurable grace to us so that in the coming ages, from now until Christ returns, and beyond, his kindness will be known. Paul declares that God's salvation plan was purposed to declare God's unmatched generosity to the ages. Most likely Paul is speaking not just about time, but about the rulers and powers that exist in that time. Christ's death and resurrection stand in stark opposition to the authorities of the present age, and God's abundant grace extended to humans leaves the spiritual forces slack-jawed in amazement. Paul reminds us here that our salvation actually has ramifications beyond our personal and corporate lives in Christ. God's plan of salvation stands as vindication of God's goodness to his creation, his commitment to his covenants and promises, and his power over all evil.

God's Masterpiece

The final verse (2:10) in this section directs the believer's vision from the heavenly realm into the world, and offers the second ramification concerning our salvation in Christ. The believers have a purpose, divinely given and divinely empowered: to function as God's agents of goodness in the world. To fully appreciate Paul's argument, we need to focus on several key terms in this verse, including his description of believers as God's masterpiece or handiwork and the good works laid out before them. And we need to address the idea of works as it relates to believers' lives of faith.

To the first point, Paul describes believers as God's masterpiece or handiwork. The term was used in the larger Greek world to speak of creative accomplishments such as composing a poem. The term carries an exalted meaning. For example, both canoes and yacht are boats, but only the latter would qualify as the kind of masterpiece of creativity Paul is signaling here. Paul has been building to this crescendo for nine verses. In this section, Paul has described believers' pasts as one of death, drowning under the weight of fleshly passions, suffocating under the power of the ruler of the air. All that changes in Christ; believers are greatly loved by God, given the gift of salvation, saved by grace, made alive with Christ, raised and seated with Christ in the heavenlies. It takes one's breath away; no wonder Paul declares that we are God's masterpiece, for God's love, care and glory come together in our salvation.

Connected with the term "handiwork" or masterpiece is the verb "to create." God's work in us can be summed up as new creation. The verb is used only with God as the subject in the New Testament, and it can reference either physical or spiritual creation. The two words are used together here to speak of the believer's new life in Christ, but they are found together in Rom 1:20, which speaks of God's physical creation of the world. We will return to the subject of physical creation in a moment, but we cannot overestimate the importance for Paul of the concept of new creation. Paul insists to the Corinthians that each of them is a new creation in Christ, using the noun form of the verb. The context is that of recognizing that all humans die, and Christ died for all. Thus if one has died in Christ, then that one is a new creation (2 Cor 5:14–17). The phrase "new creation" is found in Gal 6:15, but here the contrast is between those who advocate circumcision of the flesh, and those who cling to the cross.

Paul declares that circumcision and uncircumcision count for nothing, only the new creation matters. The reality of the new creation, then, is seen against the backdrop of both the Jew/Gentile identity struggle, and the battle between the present evil age and the age to come, inaugurated now in Christ.

Good Works

What is the function for which God's masterpieces have been created? Paul describes it as "good works," which have been laid out in advance by God. Christians from diverse traditions today for various reasons seem to have an allergic reaction to the phrase "good works." Heart rates elevate, palms sweat, and people prepare themselves for an onslaught of guilt feelings. Or perhaps eyes glaze over, minds tune out, and people figure that the whole works business is for those who don't really trust God for their salvation. Both reactions are rooted in a bifurcation of our humanity into the saved soul and the damned flesh. This gnostic view, however, could not be more inaccurate. As we saw above, salvation is for the total person. The promise of a resurrected body well suited for life on the new earth signals that our current life as a member of Christ's body provides practice for life in the age to come. I suggest that Paul understands creation as functional, that Paul cannot imagine a new creation without its attending purpose. The purpose gives value and makes sense of the created entity. A new creation without an attending purpose would be like having a golf ball with no clubs. Therefore to see the new believer's life through a template of works for merit versus saved by grace does not capture Paul's intentions here. The point is new creation, which, like the physical creation, is designed with a purpose in mind. The creature is equipped to function as it should by its Creator.

No believer needs to cast about looking for good works, for God has provided a way for each believer to fulfill his or her purpose. What is intended by Paul's claim that God has prepared good works "in advance"? It could imply that before the foundation of the world specific activities were decided upon and individuals' names were attached to each. It is also possible that Paul speaks more generally here of kingdom work which has been prepared for by Christ's death and resurrection. Jesus speaks of the fields being ready for harvest, and needing reapers (Matt 9:37). General tasks such as caring for widows and orphans (Jas 1:27), bearing each other's burdens (Gal 6:2), resisting sin (1 Cor 10:12–13), loving enemies (Luke 6:32–36), and living by the Spirit (Rom 14:17–18) are laid out in the New Testament as responsibilities to be carried out by followers of Jesus.

These behaviors, attitudes, and sympathies are to be as natural as walking. Indeed, Paul states that we are to walk in these good works. Interestingly, in 2:1, Paul indicates that the Gentiles walk in their trespasses and sins, in what amounts to a death march. But believers walk in newness of life, moving from one good, holy, blessed action or attitude to another, step by step, bringing God glory in all things. The image of the Christian life as a walk occurs frequently in Paul. He admonishes the Galatians to walk by the Spirit (5:16) and keep in step with the Spirit (5:25, see also Rom 6:4; 8:4; 2 Cor 5:2; Phil 3:17; Col 1:10). In Ephesians Paul repeatedly asks that they walk worthy of their calling (4:1, 17; 5:2, 8, 15). Some translations (including the TNIV) render the Greek as "live" rather than "walk," which might lose a bit of the sense of energy, direction, and purpose assumed in the term "walk." More so in Paul's time than now, walking was the way one supported life: people walked their animals to the fields and back home, they walked to get water, to attend synagogue or festivals, to plant and harvest crops. Life depended upon walking. Everyone knew that to walk was to live, and to live was to walk (or have a servant do the walking for you). The image of walking in the Spirit, or walking in good works, was a natural way of saying how the believer's new life, the life of a new creature, was to be nourished and maintained.

If Paul's life is anything to go on, walking in good works is hard, scary, exhilarating, and exhausting all at once. Paul does not say that God will smooth out the path, or keep the weather sunny and the wind to the back. Paul is walking, doing, being in real time under the power of the Spirit. The Spirit did not carry Paul as a parent might do for a toddler; Paul was walking, acting, choosing, but not alone. Always within, around, and beside is the God who saves—Father, Son, and Holy Spirit.

CHRIST, OUR PEACE (2:11–22)

[11]Therefore, remember that formerly you who are Gentiles by birth and called "uncircumcised" by those who call

themselves "the circumcision" (which is done in the body by human hands)—[12]remember that at that time you were separate from Christ, excluded from citizenship in Israel and foreigners to the covenants of the promise, without hope and without God in the world. [13]But now in Christ Jesus you who once were far away have been brought near by the blood of Christ. [14]For he himself is our peace, who has made the two one and has destroyed the barrier, the dividing wall of hostility, [15]by setting aside in his flesh the law with its commands and regulations. His purpose was to create in himself one new humanity out of the two, thus making peace, [16]and in one body to reconcile both of them to God through the cross, by which he put to death their hostility. [17]He came and preached peace to you who were far away and peace to those who were near. [18]For through him we both have access to the Father by one Spirit. [19]Consequently, you are no longer foreigners and strangers, but fellow citizens with God's people and also members of his household, [20]built on the foundation of the apostles and prophets, with Christ Jesus himself as the chief cornerstone. [21]In him the whole building is joined together and rises to become a holy temple in the Lord. [22]And in him you too are being built together to become a dwelling in which God lives by his Spirit.

In the second half of the chapter, Paul identifies two consequences of his previous declarations that believers (Jew and Gentile) are God's masterpiece. Both these statements are introduced by "therefore" (2:11, 19). The claims made are further elaborated upon in 2:14–18, which discusses how it is that Gentiles and Jews share in Christ. Paul's argument is more explicit and detailed here than at the beginning of the chapter, for he further defines both humanity's situation and Christ's role in God's salvation plan. To capture these twin emphases, we will look first at Paul's argument concerning Jews and Gentiles in 2:11–13, 19–22 and then focus on 2:14–18.

No Longer Strangers (2:11–13, 19–22)

Paul addresses the Ephesians directly by asking them to recall their lives before they heard the gospel message. Certain things were true, including that they were without God (2:12), although clearly most of them would have at that time retorted that they were devoted to their gods. But from Paul's (and any Jew's) perspective, Gentiles in the main did not forsake idolatry; they lived without recognizing God in their everyday lives. Again, they were strangers to all that true knowledge of God offered, including the covenants of the promise, the hope that only God brings; they were outside the community that bears God's revelation to the world. Paul describes it as alienated from the citizenship of Israel (2:12). This unique phrase is rich with subtle meaning. First, the term "citizenship" is used elsewhere only in Phil 3:20 (using a cognate term), where Paul contrasts the believer's loyalty to God and his promises of a new heavens and earth, not to earthly things which have about them the stench of death. Paul is hinting at the same truth here, that citizenship within Israel is membership into God's family. Second, Paul uses "Israel" in a specific sense here, focusing on the spiritual Israel, those Jews who know the covenants, the promise and the hope of God. Paul divides Jews into those who are circumcised in the flesh, and those who are circumcised also in the heart (see Jer 9:26). He reminds the Ephesians that they are called the uncircumcised, but that this label has been given to them by those who see things from a fleshly perspective, not those who understand that true circumcision is that which is done to the heart.

But the Gentile Ephesians remain no longer in their former state, for in Christ they are now close to God, they are now fellow citizens with the saints, they are full members of God's family, they are building pieces of God's holy temple (2:13, 19–22). Each of these images brings depth to our understanding of the Christian life. Paul declares that they are no longer outsiders, but are part of the community of saints. Because he speaks here of being fellow citizens, it is likely that the term "saints" is parallel to "Israel" in 2:12. The riches of God's kingdom life, and fellowship with those who worship the one true God, are now counted as well to Gentiles in Christ.

Fusing the Horizons: Citizenship

I take my U.S. citizenship for granted; I was born with it, did nothing to earn it.[2] Sometimes I forget that it offers certain privileges and constitutional rights. Citizenship in the ancient world was not taken for granted, indeed, it was highly prized, for few enjoyed it. Having citizenship was a way to show loyalty to Rome, and it gave Rome the opportunity to reward those who showed allegiance. Julius Caesar started an aggressive program of granting citizenship to aliens/*peregrini*. He gave Sicily Latin rights, very similar to Roman citizenship. And he would grant Roman citizenship to whole legions of *peregrini* (foreigners) as a way to enfranchise them and give them a stake in the republic. Augustus and Claudius continued the trend of offering citizenship to more groups. By 212 CE, Emperor Caracalla gave Roman citizenship to all free people in the empire.

Among the privileges of Roman citizenship was that of *conubium*, or the right to enter a licit marriage, giving offspring the rank of Roman citizen, and claim to the father's estate. Additionally, Roman citizens had the right of *jus commercii* (to own and sell property outright), and had access to Roman courts. Citizens were not to be beaten or tortured before a trial. While both women and men enjoyed these privileges, the latter benefitted from the additional rights of voting, joining the Roman legion, and holding public office. A registry of citizens' names was kept in Rome and updated approximately every five years, coordinated with the census. The names of freed slaves would be recorded in the local registry with copies sent to Rome. Similarly, a child born to a citizen would be registered within thirty days of birth, and a personal copy could be kept at their home. The official document was held in the city's public archives and perhaps in Rome as well.

How did one become a citizen? One could be born a citizen, as was Paul. Or one could purchase the privilege, as did Claudius Lysias, the tribune who questioned Paul in Jerusalem (Acts 22:26–29; 23:26). One could bribe officials to have their name placed on a list of potential citizens going up for nomination. And one could receive citizenship upon manumission from

2. Citizenship in the community of ancient Israel was similar in that it was the birthright of every Israelite to be a member of God's household, a part of the covenant community. The gospel invites Gentiles in Christ to be full members of the new community of God's people.

slavery. It is this last option that I think might resonate with Paul's metaphorical use of citizenship and slavery in his writings. Paul notes that believers are free—free from the deathly grip of sin, free from the power of the flesh, free from the constraints and restrictions of the law. Like a manumitted slave, believers now enjoy the privileges of citizenship.

We do not know how many of the Ephesian and Philippian Christians were citizens of their cities or of Rome. Philippi was a Roman colony, and many veterans with their Roman citizenship settled there. Whether these men or their families were Christian is unclear, but probably unlikely. Thus, for believers to be part of God's commonwealth, a citizen of an eternal kingdom, was good news indeed. It should be good news as well today, and the church has a special contribution to make in the conversation of citizenship. Concerning immigration and illegal aliens, the church has an opportunity to develop these hot-button issues beyond the contexts of (alleged) increased crime or jobs lost to citizens. We can critique earthly citizenship when it privileges one group over another, and we can celebrate with believers from around the globe a single citizenship in the commonwealth of God's kingdom. Paul used his Roman citizenship to advance the gospel, not to further his own rights. As he notes in his letter to the Ephesians, he is chained to a Roman soldier (3:1; 4:1; 6:20); with a single word denying Christ, Paul would be a free man with all the privileges and honor that his Roman citizenship carries. Instead, he sees his Roman citizenship as an opportunity to introduce Jesus and his eternal citizenship to as many people as would listen. He held his Roman citizenship lightly because he knew it was of the present age which is passing away. He clung to his citizenship in heaven, knowing it would outlast time.

In celebrating the new life in Christ, Paul draws on Isaiah's promise (Isa 57:19), which pictures God's peace extended to the lowly and contrite, whether near or far. Isaiah warns, however, that the wicked will have no peace. It is perhaps no accident that after declaring that those far off have been brought near through Christ's blood (see also 1:7), Paul's next statement is that Christ is our peace.

He Is Our Peace (2:14–18)

What does it mean that Christ is our peace? Note that Paul does not say that Christ is "your" peace, as though Christ's work is sufficient or necessary only for Gentiles. Rather, Christ's work is effective for both Jew and Gentile. Both Jew and Gentile are necessary for us to understand the full ramifications of Christ's work. For Paul, Christ takes two entities and makes them one new thing. This happens in nature when an egg and a sperm meet and create something new. We see it in the description of marriage in Gen 2:24, that a woman and a man come together in marriage and are then legally and socially a new entity (5:29–32, see also 1 Cor 6:16). We must avoid concluding that Christ acts as a United Nations negotiator who keeps two countries or factions from fighting. This scenario assumes a power differential that manages to keep chaos at bay. Additionally, the difference represented in the Jews and Gentiles is not merely a tribal, ethnic, or a national struggle, but a spiritual struggle centering on the identity of the people of God. The peace that Christ brings is not the absence of hostilities, or even the willingness to tolerate the other. In Christ, there is no "other."

The term "peace" is complex, having a range of meaning. The context is crucial. In the New Testament it can mean absence of war (Rev 6:4) or calmness of mind (Col 3:15); or it can identify a characteristic of God, "God of peace" (Rom 15:33), "peace of Christ" (Col 3:15); or it can name a fruit of the Spirit (Gal 5:22–23). Paul's greetings include his wish that his readers experience the grace and peace of God. Paul explains in Rom 5:1 that we have peace with God, having been justified through the death and resurrection of the Lord Jesus (Rom 4:25). Such good news is expressed in the Gospels as well. Luke records the angels' song at Jesus' birth that proclaims peace on earth (Luke 2:14). Jesus declared in the Beatitudes that peacemakers are blessed; they will be called the children of God (Matt 5:9). In John's Gospel, Jesus pronounces that he brings peace, and that in him is peace (16:33; 14:27). Again, and not without irony, Peter declares to Cornelius, a Roman centurion who makes his living as a soldier, that the gospel is the good news of peace through Jesus Christ which God sent to his people Israel (Acts 10:36). In Ephesians, "peace" is declared, for the hostilities between Jew and Gentile have been stilled in Christ—the two are now one. And this is not only in personal attitude or individual actions; peace is to be a lived reality as the church gathers in one place to worship the one Lord. As our peace, Christ makes Gentiles fellow heirs, fellow citizens with Jews in God's commonwealth.

One final note—a question really. Why did not Paul write that Christ is our salvation? Surely that is what he meant, right? Once again, however,

Paul is encouraging his readers to take in the full effect of their reconciliation through Christ's cross. Salvation is not simply a vertical relationship between God and humans that is restored and enhanced, to which an ultimately optional horizontal aspect is added. This false dichotomy separates what in Paul's mind is a unity.[3] The relationship believers have with God in Christ is evidenced by living the new creation life here and now. No new creation, no reconciliation. God is intent on redeeming and reconciling all creation, including his image bearers (humans) who by faith are in Christ.

Christ Breaks Down the Dividing Wall

Paul builds his argument by explaining that Christ has done three things: he has made the two one, he has broken down the dividing wall, and he has annulled the law of the commandments. Taking a closer look at these accomplishments, we can be comfortably sure that the two entities made one are Jew and Gentile, but the dividing wall is more difficult to interpret. Perhaps Paul is constructing a metaphor that will interact with a second picture at the end of the chapter, namely the building up of God's temple (2:21–22). It is also possible that Paul is alluding to the wall of separation in the Jerusalem temple. The difficulty is that Paul uses two terms for this wall; he speaks of the middle wall of the fence, wall, or barrier. Why use such an elaborate phrase? Perhaps it is referencing a specific image, such as the barrier that excludes Gentiles from the Jewish area of the temple. This wall was in the midst of the temple precinct, hence it might be described as a "middle wall." It also served as a barrier or fence to keep out the ritually unclean (Gentiles) from a pure, sacred space reserved for Jews.[4]

Although this wall still stood in Paul's day, he insists that in Christ both Jew and Gentile have full access to God. Paul probably preached something of the sort, if accusations against him are anything to go on. In Acts 21:28–29, certain Jews from the province of Asia (Ephesus is located here) accuse Paul of bringing Greeks into the temple, thereby defiling it. Since Gentiles were permitted in the outer court of the temple, the accusation must be alleging that Paul took Gentiles beyond the barrier. Such an

3. Wright 2009: 126–27.
4. Josephus *Ant.* 15.417.

act would have resulted in the defiling Gentile's death. Why might such an accusation be leveled against Paul, unless he in fact taught that in Christ no barrier existed? I am not suggesting that Paul violated the temple or would put at risk one of his fellow believers. But in his teachings, it is likely that Paul contrasted the physical barriers of the Jerusalem temple with what all believers now have in Christ, namely full access to the Father through the blood of the Son. Nor am I suggesting that Paul wants to give Gentiles the same access to the temple as the Jews had—this was the mistake made by his accusers, and reveals their narrow vision. Paul does not promote equal opportunity for Gentiles, for that would tacitly accept the present system with minor (though important) variations. In Christ, the entire system of Law, temple, and sacrifice is rendered obsolete. The point is that a new person now exists where once there was Jew and Gentile. The promises of God have their fulfillment. The new person is a preview of the new creation, the new heavens and new earth. With Christ's death and resurrection, with the filling of the Spirit, the believer is now part of the new creation.

The Term "Hostility" in Paul's Argument

Equally difficult to understand is Paul's comment concerning the law of the commandments in ordinances, and its relationship to what precedes it: "the hostility in his flesh." We are left to decide Paul's intentions based on grammar rules, which can be broken. Certain questions need answered, including whether the term "hostility" should be understood to explain the dividing wall and whether this wall was broken in his flesh, or whether the law was abolished in his flesh. Additionally, we must explore why Paul described the law with further qualifiers "commands" and "regulations."

To the first set of issues, the questions revolve around whether the phrase "the hostility in his flesh" connects with the previous participle "having broken down" or with the following participle "having annulled or abrogated." One possible reading is to connect "hostility" with the preceding dividing wall as a further descriptor. This hostility would then be destroyed or broken down. However, it is not typical for modifiers to be on both sides of a participle. This implies a second, more likely reading, where "hostility" would further define the law of the commandments. A related question is the place of the phrase "in his flesh." It might refer back to the dividing wall which was destroyed "in his flesh." But that syntax is awkward. Additionally, some argue that to say Christ's work in the flesh destroyed enmity between Jew and Gentile is too narrow an interpretation of Christ's death. However, as I noted above, Paul understands reconciliation with God and new creation as two sides of the same coin, both gained through Christ's death and resurrection. Nonetheless, it makes most sense to include "in his flesh" with the abrogation of the law, the third participle in the grouping. In sum, we suggest that both "hostility" and "in his flesh" are connected with the annulment of the law. Paul is thus arguing that the hostility between Jews and Gentiles that is generated by the law (more on this below) is annulled or made inoperative in Christ's flesh, probably referring to his death on the cross (2:13).

Why does Paul qualify the noun "law" with the phrase "with its commands and regulations"? It is historically anachronistic to divide the law into moral and ceremonial categories; Paul would not have been thinking in such terms. However, if the dividing wall points metaphorically to the temple barrier, then the law of commandments in ordinances might also speak to those decrees in particular that limit Jew/Gentile interaction, namely circumcision (mentioned in 2:11) and food laws (see Gal 2:12–13) and even Sabbath (as in Rom 14:5–6). These rites which create barriers between Jew and Gentile do not qualify as the covenants of the promise (2:12). Again, Paul claims to the Galatians that if the Gentile men among them get circumcised, then they are obliged the keep the entire law (Gal 5:3). Less likely is the possibility that the term "regulations" does not go with commandments, but is contrasted to them. Thus Paul would be arguing that in Christ's ordinances, the law of the commandments has been annulled, similar to his argument in 2 Cor 3:7–18, which contrasts the written code and the ministry of the Spirit.[5]

In any case, what is clear is that the law no longer has the power to divide. Moreover, Christ's purpose is to make something new from what were once two. This new thing is his body, the church, which now has access in Christ to God the Father through the Spirit. The cross is not only the place where believers' sins are forgiven, but also the place where something new is created. The new creation is not simply a new individual, but a new entity—Christ's body, the church. As noted above, this new entity can be described as God's household and God's temple

---

5. Heine 2002: 135–36, quoting Origen.

where his Spirit dwells. This amazing reality is especially poignant to Paul, because he wears chains testifying to its truthfulness. In the next chapter Paul puts his own situation into perspective, given the surpassing greatness of the reality he and all believers share in Christ through the Spirit to God the Father.

EPHESIANS 3

After the heavy theological lifting of chs. 1 and 2, ch. 3 carries a slower, more repetitive pace. It is as though, having chugged steadily up the steep theological hill, Paul is pausing a bit to allow his readers to catch their breath, before plunging on with his exhortations in chs. 4–6. Key terms and phrases are carried over or expanded. For example, Paul repeats the foundational importance of the apostles and prophets, and further describes the unique, amazing composition of God's church—Jew and Gentile together in Christ. In ch. 3, Paul describes how his personal story is related to the gospel message explained in the preceding chapters. He also highlights one ramification of God's marvelous plan of redemption—that we (Jew and Gentile) may freely and confidently pray to God with utter assurance of being welcomed and heard (3:12). From a structural standpoint, ch. 3 can be divided in half, with the first section concerned with Paul's self-description and the second with Paul's prayer for the Ephesians. Paul explains his potentially shameful position of being in chains as glorious for the Gentiles in light of God's redemptive work in Christ. His prayer centers on the reality of the new, inner person who is created in Christ from every family (both Jew and Gentile). Paul prays that this new believer might be saturated inside and out to the bursting point with Christ's love and God's fullness.

PAUL, A PRISONER IN CHAINS (3:1–13)

¹For this reason I, Paul, the prisoner of Christ Jesus for the sake of you Gentiles—²Surely you have heard about the administration of God's grace that was given to me for you, ³that is, the mystery made known to me by revelation, as I have already written briefly. ⁴In reading this, then, you will be able to understand my insight into the mystery of Christ, ⁵which was not made known to people in other generations

as it has now been revealed by the Spirit to God's holy apostles and prophets. [6]This mystery is that through the gospel the Gentiles are heirs together with Israel, members together of one body, and sharers together in the promise in Christ Jesus. [7]I became a servant of this gospel by the gift of God's grace given me through the working of his power. [8]Although I am less than the least of all the Lord's people, this grace was given me: to preach to the Gentiles the boundless riches of Christ, [9]and to make plain to everyone the administration of this mystery, which for ages past was kept hidden in God, who created all things. [10]His intent was that now, through the church, the manifold wisdom of God should be made known to the rulers and authorities in the heavenly realms, [11]according to his eternal purpose that he accomplished in Christ Jesus our Lord. [12]In him and through faith in him we may approach God with freedom and confidence. [13]I ask you, therefore, not to be discouraged because of my sufferings for you, which are your glory.

Paul's Rhetorical Strategy

Paul's self-description here in the first half of chapter 3 can be understood as a digression from his argument in 2:22 which he then picks up again in 3:14. If 3:1–13 were missing, Paul's argument would flow nicely from his mention of Gentiles being members of God's household (2:19) to his prayer to the Father from whom every family takes its name (3:14). After declaring that Gentiles and Jews are being built together into God's dwelling place (2:22), his prayer that Christ would dwell in their hearts follows naturally (3:17). An obvious question to raise, then, is why Paul included 3:1–13. For the answer, it seems best to turn to the ancient modes of rhetoric, the art of persuasion. Although rhetoric today carries negative connotations, in Paul's time it suggested the educated speech of one who sought to convince his audience of the right decision, attitude, or behavior. Orators sought to connect with their audience as part of the persuasive task, realizing that sometimes logic alone would not generate sufficient passion within the audience for the requested tasks. A digression might serve such a function, as well as introduce pertinent and relevant information that, while not necessarily logically related to the specific argument, would advance the overall agenda. Quintilian notes that a digression highlights a relevant theme important to the overall case being discussed.[1] Moreover, the digression is usually in the form of epideictic rhetoric, that is, it concerns praise or blame. These characteristics are found in Paul's digression.

Paul's strategy of using a digression is rooted in his choice of argument style. Typically the rhetor would begin with a prologue (*exordium*), next offer a report of the situation, often with a historical glance backwards (*narratio*), then provide the logical argument of his case (*argumentatio*), and conclude with a summary of the argument that also sought to reconnect with the audience (*peroratio*). Usually the argument is based on the preceding explanation of the situation, and includes the consequences of following (or not) the line of reasoning. However, Paul does not threaten the Ephesians with dire consequences if they fail to live holy lives or promise great reward if they do. Rather, he exhorts and encourages them to walk worthy of who they are in Christ. Thus we might conclude that rather than using the *argumentatio*, Paul employs the rhetorical category of *exhortatio* in chapters 4–6. With this strategy, Paul seeks to persuade the Ephesians of the truth of his ideas and the reality of its relevance to their own lives, rather than working within the framework of logic. Indeed, the gospel itself, Paul declares, is mysterious and beyond human wisdom, so that human logic would fail to fully grasp or appreciate the gospel's fullness. We might conclude that "the ethical concern explicit in the *exhortatio* is implicit in the *exordium/narratio* of chapters 1–3."[2] In this reconstruction of Paul's argument, then, his digression serves the necessary purpose of connecting deeply with his audience, gaining their good will and sympathy, before asking for concrete behaviors and attitudes from his congregants.

In 3:1–13, Paul prepares for the exhortation in the next three chapters by building rapport, emphasizing that his authority is based on his noble character and gifting from God, not on his rank or status as an apostle. Paul identifies himself as a prisoner, a minister or servant, and less than the least of God's saints. These roles or positions are all for the

---

1. Quintilian *Inst.* 4.3.14.
2. Jeal 2000: 71.

sake of the Gentiles to whom he preaches the mystery of God's redemption in Christ.

Paul's Personal Character Revealed by His Chains

Based on Paul's statement in 3:13, part of his reasoning for emphasizing his imprisonment is to reassure the Ephesians. But he does more than that, offering a robust theological argument about the value of his situation. In 3:1 he declares that he is a prisoner, not of Rome (which he is at one level), but of Christ. His point is that the physical chains that link him to a Roman soldier tell the story not of a plan gone horribly wrong, but of the wisdom of the Creator God who has orchestrated redemption of all people through Christ. He makes this point by introducing his imprisonment with the phrase "for this reason." This transitional clause points backwards to chapter 2 and its astonishing claims that Gentiles are fellow citizens with God's people, they are members of God's household, and they are part of God's temple. Paul's imprisonment is a testimony to his faithful declaration of Christ's work in making the two one, bringing together Jew and Gentile. Most likely the Ephesians would have known that Paul was accused of bringing a Gentile into the area of the Jerusalem temple reserved for Jews (Acts 21:27–29). It was this charge that started the years-long imprisonment beginning in Caesarea and ending in Rome (Acts 28:30–31). Though Paul was innocent of those specific charges, he freely admitted he was guilty of teaching that through Christ Gentiles were now part of God's people. His chains testify to his steadfast, unwavering commitment to God's appointment to preach this good news.

His chains, in other words, are the physical evidence that he is a trusted minister of God, willing to face any affliction for the truth that Gentiles are fellow heirs with Jews in God's household. His character is praiseworthy in that he fulfills his responsibilities before God in preaching the gospel to them. In the ancient world, a teacher must be morally upright, for the students were to model their lives on their teacher's example. Paul asks the Corinthians to follow his lead, as he follows Christ (1 Cor 11:1). He points to his own behavior among the Thessalonians as worthy of imitation (1 Thes 2:4–12). The Ephesians likewise would appreciate that Paul modeled for them the proper posture before God. They would feel sympathetic towards and attached to Paul, knowing that he was willing to undergo hardships on their behalf.

Fusing the Horizons: Prison Ministry Then and Now

Paul had visitors helping him cope with his house arrest and confinement, including Epaphroditus from Philippi (Phil 2:25–30). They brought food, companionship, and facilitated Paul's continuing ministry to the churches. But it would be many centuries before Christians showed an interest in prison conditions. In the early 1800s, Elizabeth Fry took up the challenge. Raised a Quaker, she desired that the Scriptures and the inner light of Christ guide her. She was married with several children when asked by a friend to visit Newgate prison, a hellhole in the midst of London. She was appalled at the conditions in which the female prisoners existed, and immediately began to organize aid. She brought clothing, established a chapel, began an education program, and instituted Bible reading. She developed a prison management system of matrons and supervisors, and established compulsory sewing. She promoted her reforms both to Parliament and in towns throughout Britain, and extended her vision to include workhouses, mental asylums, and hospitals. In the midst of her work and personal hardship, she wrote "how have the gospel truths opened gradually on my view, the height, the depth, length and breadth of the love of God in Christ Jesus, to my unspeakable help and consolation."[3] Her concerns both for prison conditions and prisoner education continue today. Prison Fellowship, begun by Chuck Colson in 1976, is one of many Christian prison ministries that embrace the words of Jesus, "I was in prison and you came to visit me" (Matt 25:36). Jesus' focus here is likely those believers imprisoned for preaching the good news. Today many Christian groups extend the mission to all prisoners, following Christ's general call to have compassion on the vulnerable in society.

Paul, a Servant

Additionally, Paul calls himself a servant (*diakonos*, 3:7) and the least of the lowest of the saints (3:8). With so many churches named for St. Paul today, we are tempted to hear false modesty in these claims. However, Paul on other occasions identified himself as God's slave (*doulos*). Again, when speaking about his apostleship to the Corinthians, he notes that he was the least of the apostles, using a word often translated "as one

3. Skidmore 2005: 158.

abnormally born" (1 Cor 15:8). The Greek term carries the sense of a spontaneously aborted fetus, misshapen and deformed. Nonetheless, he declares, God's grace to him is not in vain. So too here to the Ephesians, Paul contrasts his own unworthiness with the superior grace extended to him by God for the task of preaching to the Gentiles. Paul reinforces his conviction that the message of redemption is not based on his personal skills, but on the wealth of God's grace expressed in Paul's gospel message. In sum, Paul's hope to persuade his readers in chs. 4–6 to change their behavior or continue along the path of right living would be seriously compromised if he could not generate motivation for change. Paul's reflection on his ministry and his imprisonment serves the very necessary purpose of establishing an intimate relationship with his readers.

Fusing the Horizons: Paul the Servant

Paul declares himself a servant in 3:7. Since the 1970s, it has been popular to think of Christian leaders as "servant leaders." However, the term was coined by a business consultant, Robert Greenleaf, to promote a less autocratic corporation environment. Many in the church took over the term, using it to explain what biblical leadership looks like. But is this term best suited to describe what the Bible means about service, about leadership? Note that Paul does not describe himself as a servant leader. Nowhere in Eph 3 does he mention leadership, generally understood as giving orders or making decisions for the group. Instead, Paul stresses that a certain grace was extended to him for a specific purpose, namely to preach the mystery now made known, that Gentiles are co-heirs with Jews in Christ. This message was revealed to the apostles and prophets (3:5). Interestingly, Paul does not include himself as a member of this group, although he does identify himself as an apostle in 1:1. Perhaps in 3:5 Paul is thinking of the earliest apostles and prophets who knew Jesus' earthly ministry. This group is called upon as corroborating evidence for Paul's gospel claims. Additionally, I think Paul is teasing out his own view of apostleship, namely that it involves not leadership *per se*, but service of the most menial sort—such as seemingly wasting away chained to a Roman soldier. Such servant behavior shows most clearly the powerful grace of God, and it glorifies those whom it serves.

The Mystery of Christ

Knowing why he offered this personal description provides the platform to look more deeply into the content. Only three sentences in Greek, 3:2–13 interrupt his opening lines in 3:1. Verses 2–7 reflect on Paul's position as a prisoner and the mystery of God's redemption from one angle, and vv. 8–12 pick up both emphases from a second viewpoint. In both cases, Paul builds on the theological claims of the previous chapter, further reflecting on the images of believers (Jew and Gentile) as the body of Christ, as the household of God, and as the holy temple to the Lord. Verse 3:13 offers a reason for the digression, namely that his Gentile congregants would not despair of his situation, but take heart that his chains and afflictions are actually evidence of God's redemption in Christ extended to Gentiles. But the digression not only builds rapport between Paul and the Ephesians, it also draws out implications of his previous claims of unity of Jew and Gentile in Christ. The vehicle that carries much of this thought is the term "mystery."

Paul uses the term "mystery" three times in this chapter, as well as in 1:9; 5:25; and 6:19. In 3:6 Paul states clearly that the mystery he received by revelation (3:3) is the redemption plan of God that includes Gentiles with Israel as co-heirs in Christ of God's promises. Quite simply, the mystery is the gospel, the work of Christ for the salvation of both Jew and Gentile by faith. Additionally, Paul was commissioned by the Lord to speak to the Gentiles (Acts 22:21; Gal 2:9). Nor is this gospel message Paul's private interpretation of God's mystery; the holy apostles and prophets (the foundation of the church, 2:20) were given this revelation (3:5). But to see this mystery as only concerning personal salvation is to miss the bigger picture. Paul hints at this in chapter 1, where he introduces the term in the phrase "mystery of his will," that is, God's purpose that redemption of all things is through Christ (1:9–10). Again, Paul explains that the revelation of this mystery results in the church bearing witness of God's multifaceted wisdom to the heavenly powers and principalities (3:10). Key to the mystery is the oneness of the church, which is further emphasized in 5:25, as Paul compares the oneness of a married couple to that union of Christ and his church.

Paul uses "mystery" in similar ways in other epistles. In Rom 11:25 Paul speaks of the mystery of Israel's hardening until the full number of Gentiles is included. Again, in 16:25–26, Paul stresses the revelation of the mystery previously hidden but now made manifest through the prophetic scriptures. This doxological setting is similar to Eph 1:9. Both passages in Romans stress God's work through Christ to the Gentiles. Colossians 1:27 likewise stresses the important of Gentile inclusion in God's household, while 2:2 identifies the mystery as Christ himself, who contains all wisdom and knowledge. This aspect of the term "mystery" is similar to Paul's discussion in 1 Cor 2:7, where Paul describes God's wisdom as a mystery. The content of God's wisdom was explained in the previous chapter as the cross of Christ and its power to save. Paul continues that the wisdom found in Christ is that which redeems and sanctifies (1 Cor 1:30). Further in 1 Corinthians the term "mystery" carries an eschatological sense, as he notes the mystery of the second coming when all believers will be changed (1 Cor 15:51). While the nuances of each letter shape Paul's specific meaning of "mystery," overall the term carries the sense that God's work in Christ, now revealed in the gospel message, promotes the full inclusion of Gentiles into God's household. Elsewhere Paul focuses more on Christ's work of redemption, which stresses both Israel and Gentiles; in Ephesians, the spotlight shines on the reality of Gentile joined with Jew in Christ's body.

Paul declares that the mystery of God was previously hidden, but is now revealed. He states that people in the past did not know this mystery, and by this he does not mean that they were ignorant of God or his will. God's revelation in the Law and through the prophets, promises, and covenants all stand as a testimony to the believer (1 Cor 10:6; Rom 9:4–5). Paul intends here a very specific claim, namely that God's work to redeem Gentiles *as Gentiles* and not as proselytes to Judaism is the mysterious, glorious, unexpected aspect of God's redemptive plan. Rather than wait for the *eschaton* to bring believing Gentiles (God-fearers like Cornelius, Acts 10:1–3, 47) into the fold, God in Christ has brought redemption in the present age. This greatest work of grace was not revealed fully to the faithful of Israel in the past, although what was revealed is instructive for the church (Rom 15:4). But now the apostles and prophets of the church testify to God's redeeming grace in Christ. They did not invent the message rather it was given by the Spirit through revelation (3:5).

Gentiles and Jews Together in Christ

Today many think in the binary categories "saved" and "not saved." Another binary category often used today is that of horizontal and vertical dimensions of salvation, what we call ecclesiology and soteriology, with the latter taking precedent over the former. Relying on such a lens, however, for Ephesians can prevent us from appreciating Paul's claims. Paul emphasizes the Jew/Gentile division for both historical and theological reasons. Historically, the division was imposed by his circumstances; Jews worshiped the one true God in Jerusalem, and everyone else was without God in the world. From Paul's Jewish perspective this partition represents a greater social or ethnic divide than existed among the many Gentile groups (Egyptian, Greek, Persian, etc.). If Christ is able to break down the heavily fortified social walls between Jew and Gentile, certainly the ethnic tensions between Greek and Scythian, or Egyptian and Roman, could be resolved in Christ as well.

But underpinning this historical reality was a deeper theological division between the people of God and idolaters. These opposite groups face different struggles in their coming to God. We saw in 2:1–3 that Gentiles were without hope and without God, wasting away in their pagan futility, while Jews were trapped by the flesh, the pull of sinful desires which battle against God's call to holiness as outlined in his Law. Two points should be emphasized. First, the distinctions between Jew and Gentile cannot be reduced to racial tension, although in the ancient world racial tensions between all sorts of groups, including Jews with others, did flare up in various cities across the Empire. For Paul, however, the theological distinctions are crucial—the Jews are the people of God based on God's covenants and promises and thus are not simply an ethnic group, but they carry with them the revelation of the true God. We must take care, then, today when drawing parallels with current ethnic tensions or racial issues. These analogies are useful but somewhat limited in that no two other groups today carry the theological weight of the Jew/Gentile division.

Second, our understanding of salvation should not be divided into vertical and horizontal halves, for in Christ, there is both vertical and horizontal, or there is nothing. Until Christ, the people of God were identified based on their relationship to God's covenants and promises, including that of circumcision. In Christ, the Gentile, the idolater, is made new from the inside out, and is placed in God's family. So often we stop at the first clause—the idolater was made new—and downplay or even ignore the second half—they are part of God's household. But Paul does not separate them. Salvation, for Paul, is not understandable outside one's changed status as a member of God's people. Breaking down the dividing wall between Jew and Gentile and making the two one signals the ultimate destruction of the principalities and powers. In this unity, the church stands against the powers of this age. This means that ecclesiology is not a secondary matter, but central to the proclamation of God's victory over sin and the grave. God's plan was not merely to save souls—that is the Gnostic and the Stoic hope which downplayed the physical world. Nor was God's plan merely to save individuals—that is the trap many contemporary Evangelicals fall into. Rather God's plan, as outlined by Paul in Ephesians, is to establish a new body, to make a new people, to build a new temple or dwelling place made up of believers both locally and across the world. The corporate body of Christ image loses its power when we think of salvation in individualistic terms. Perhaps nowhere is this clearer than in 3:10, where Paul declares that the church is God's vehicle in broadcasting his wisdom to the powers and principalities.

The ramifications of this claim are astounding; three deserve mention. First, it gives a central role to the Holy Spirit, who empowers the new community. With Christ's resurrection comes the Spirit, so that believers are not left orphans (John 14:15–18) but have the seal of God upon them, assuring them of the gospel truth (Eph 1:13–14). While few would openly state that the Holy Spirit is the least important Person of the Trinity, it happens that the work of the Spirit in making daily life within the church possible is often overlooked. But Paul stresses that believers together are God's dwelling place, a temple "in which God lives by his Spirit" (2:22). It is the presence of the Spirit presupposed in 3:10 that is seen by the rulers and authorities in the heavens. A similar claim is made in 1 Cor 3:10–17, which explains that each community of believers is blessed with the presence of the Spirit. God signifies victory over sin and death by means of a new community of the faithful, a community led by the Spirit—who signals to the powers and principalities their ultimate demise. In Eph 3:6–11, the mystery of Christ is that his people, though not ethnically similar, are all children of the promise, sealed by the Spirit. When the powers and principalities see this, they realize their days are numbered (more on the powers in ch. 6).

Second, the inextricable blending of the horizontal and vertical helps interpret Paul's claims about doing good works which God laid out in advance (Eph 2:10). If we see salvation by faith as individualistic only, then we imagine these works to be moral deeds, and we wonder about the extent of our participation with God in doing them. But if we understand salvation to include innately the creation of the new people of God, then the good works are those done by the church as it stands as light in the surrounding darkness. This amazing new community presents to the dark world the awesome power of God to break seemingly unassailable boundaries and create a new, holy, people united with bonds incomprehensible through human wisdom. Paul speaks similarly in Phil 1:27–30, when he asks the church to strive together as one body in faith, standing firm against those in Philippi who oppose them. Paul connects their struggles with his own, and as we know from Ephesians, these include his imprisonment, which is traceable to his teachings on the oneness of Jew and Gentile in Christ. Paul declares to the Philippians that their steadfastness in the Spirit signals to their opponents the latter's ultimate demise. It also reveals the Philippians' secure hope. "The reunion of the scattered fragments of humanity in the Messiah is the sign to the world that here we have nothing short of new creation."[4]

The building up of God's kingdom, taking God's light to darkness and standing fast, is organically connected to one's status as a child of God. The missional aspect of salvation is not optional. Dietrich Bonhoeffer reflected on this subject while imprisoned by the Nazis. He writes to Eberhard Bethge (June 27, 1944):

> The decisive factor is said to be that in Christianity the hope of resurrection is proclaimed, and that that means the emergence of a genuine religion of redemption, the main emphasis now being on the far side of the boundary drawn by death. But it seems to me that this is just where the mistake and the danger lie. Redemption now means redemption from cares, distress, fears, and longings, from sin and death, in a better world beyond the grave. But is this really the essential character of the proclamation of Christ in the gospels and by Paul? I should say it is not. The difference between the Christian hope of resurrection and the mythological hope is that the former sends a man back to his life on earth in a wholly new way which is even more sharply defined than it is in the Old

4. Wright 2009: 169.

Testament. The Christian, unlike the devotees of the redemption myths, has no last line of escape available from earthly tasks and difficulties into the eternal, but, like Christ himself ("my God, why hast thou forsaken me?"), he must drink the earthly cup to the dregs, and only in his doing so is the crucified and risen Lord with him, and he crucified and risen with Christ. This world must not be prematurely written off; in this the Old and New Testaments are at one. Redemption myths arise from human boundary-experiences, but Christ takes hold of a man at the centre of his life.[5]

Third, the importance of the church as the corporate body of Christ intrinsic to our salvation helps shape our understanding of forgiveness. Often forgiveness is seen as limited to that which is extended by God to believers. But the blood of Christ not only forgives sins, it makes a new community where old value assessments are turned on their heads or tossed out the window. The forgiveness is not just shown by the empty tomb but also in the new community. And because this is a new community by the Spirit, both Jews and Gentiles are equal members. Paul does not preach a "gospel" message and then tack onto it an optional picture of a multi-cultural church. Instead, the gospel message in Ephesians unfolds by stressing forgiveness of sins through Christ's blood (1:7) as a mystery (1:9), which in 3:3–10 is further explained as Gentiles becoming heirs with Jews in Christ. Forgiveness includes not simply a "not guilty" stamp, but also a new group identity. This reality is an inseparable part of the gospel message, not an optional politically correct stance. A unified diverse church is God's plan of redemption.

In 3:13, Paul asks his readers not to despair due to his afflictions, for these sufferings are their glory.[6] Notice Paul does not say *for* your glory. Paul invites us to ponder the connection between his afflictions and glory, as well as prepares the reader for his doxological prayer that highlights God's glory. Paul's afflictions are tied directly to his ministry as an apostle to the Gentiles. Paul's imprisonment both testified to his faithful proclamation of the gospel, and worried the Ephesians that a similar fate might await them too. While Paul does not hide the reality of Christian suffering, he also indicates that as an apostle, his call to suffer for Christ was part of the job description (1 Cor 4:9; 2 Cor 11:16–33; 12:11–12). Interestingly,

5. Bonhoeffer 1997: 336–37.

6. A less likely reading is that Paul is asking God that he himself will not get discouraged.

though Paul speaks of his afflictions (plural), he uses a singular pronoun when he writes that "it [the sufferings] is your glory." Perhaps Paul sees his apostolic ministry as a single event of suffering, as he expresses in 2 Tim 4:6, "for I am already being poured out as a drink offering."

Paul connects the honor the Ephesians now enjoy as new creatures in Christ with his afflictions. The term "glory" carries the basic meaning of a "summation of all of one's attributes and thus one's reputation and/or honor."[7] Usually "glory" primarily refers to God's glory (but see 1 Cor 11:7), which invites the question as to why Paul would speak of the Ephesians' glory. Their glory is in and for Christ, just as Paul's suffering is in and for Christ. A similar sentiment is expressed in Rom 8:17–18 and 2 Cor 4:17. In Rom 8:18, he notes that the sufferings experienced by Christians in the present age will not compare with "the glory that will be revealed in us." Such suffering identifies believers as in Christ, for they are participating, as did Christ, in suffering endemic to this age. As co-heirs with Christ, they will share in his glory when all is revealed, in the day of the redemption of their bodies (Rom 8:23). In 2 Cor 4:17 Paul comforts the Corinthians in the hope that "our light and momentary troubles are achieving for us an eternal glory that far outweighs them all." This eternal glory that is the believer's own in Christ comes at the cost of Christ's death and the church's suffering. For Paul specifically, it comes with the responsibilities of apostleship. Col 1:24–26 reflects a similar idea as well. Here Paul indicates that he rejoices in his suffering for the Colossians, that as Christ's servant commissioned to preach "the word of God in its fullness" he presents the mystery of the gospel, which is "Christ in you, the hope of glory." In both Colossians and Ephesians, Paul reflects on how his imprisonment and his other afflictions have testified to the mystery of the gospel, that Christ died and was raised for both Jew and Gentile. To conclude, then, in Eph 3:13 the Gentiles enjoy a share in Christ's glory through the gospel, which is preached to them by Paul, who remains a prisoner because of his calling. The afflictions he suffers for the sake of the gospel are evidence of the profound truth that Gentiles are members of God's family, and thus share in God's glory through Christ.

7. Hoehner 2002: 469.

PAUL'S PRAYER AND DOXOLOGY (3:14–21)

> [14]For this reason I kneel before the Father, [15]from whom every family in heaven and on earth derives its name. [16]I pray that out of his glorious riches he may strengthen you with power through his Spirit in your inner being, [17]so that Christ may dwell in your hearts through faith. And I pray that you, being rooted and established in love, [18]may have power, together with all the Lord's people, to grasp how wide and long and high and deep is the love of Christ, [19]and to know this love that surpasses knowledge—that you may be filled to the measure of all the fullness of God. [20]Now to him who is able to do immeasurably more than all we ask or imagine, according to his power that is at work within us, [21]to him be glory in the church and in Christ Jesus throughout all generations, for ever and ever! Amen.

Paul's digression in 3:1–13 lays the groundwork for his prayer for the Ephesian church. In this prayer, several concerns that he raises in the previous verses come into play. His concern for glory, for the church, and for the power of God to be working in and through them link with his explanation of God's working in his own life. Paul has shown the Ephesians in the previous chapters the redemption plan of God enacted in Christ and sealed by the Spirit. These amazing realities, however, are not merely facts to be known for the final exam that, if passed, gets us into heaven. Instead, Paul recognizes that these truths must come alive in the church and in each believer's heart and mind, thereby providing the energy to be faithful, to be the church to and for the world. Paul's prayer swells from a desire that the Ephesians might experience the reality of God's fullness in the redeemed life.

God the Father of All Families (3:14–15)

Paul offers this prayer before he begins his requests for their behavior changes in 4:1. Often we reverse the order; we demand change, and then pray that it happens. Paul's approach is instructive; it signals that any hoped for behavior or attitude change has to be rooted in the convictions that God wants the holy lifestyle and is more than capable of supplying the power to live out the new life in Christ. Additionally, it shows the Ephesians that Paul's upcoming requests are not pie-in-the-sky impossible dreams that only few super-spiritual people can achieve. Instead, in hearing Paul's prayer, each believer is assured the reality of God's power in their inner person, the Spirit working and Christ dwelling, so that new life flows naturally from their changed nature or status.

Paul describes his posture—kneeling—rather than stating directly that he is praying. This vivid word picture has Old Testament resonances for Paul. In Rom 14:11 and Phil 2:10, Paul draws on Isa 45:23 in his convictions that every knee will bow to honor Christ and God the Father (see also Rom 11:4, citing 1 Kgs 19:18). Some suggest that the hymn in Phil 2:5–11 was well known to Paul's churches. If the Ephesians were also aware of it, Paul's posture before God would call to mind the promised victory of Christ. Paul presents a picture of humility, but also one of tremendous hope, for his bowed knee foreshadows the eschatological event where all render appropriate obeisance to God. It is unclear whether earliest Christians often knelt in prayer, but perhaps the physical act of kneeling today would be a useful reminder to believers of the eschatological event in which God's majesty will be honored by all.

Paul kneels before God the Father, a common appellation for God in this letter. Most likely Paul uses it here because he wants to draw a wordplay on that name (*pater*) and the term for family (*patria*). Every family, those on earth and in heaven, draws their name from God. Paul likely intends here that every human clan is ultimately from God, as God is the creator of all (3:9). But what does Paul imply by speaking of every family in heaven? Some argue he is referring to angels, although it would seem an odd way to do so, as angels are not grouped as families. A better option is that Paul is asserting that, in the end, separation by death (with the dead in heaven and others remaining on earth) does not divide families. Does this mean that Paul is thinking only of redeemed families? Not necessarily; rather he presents the conviction that every family comes under God's redemptive plan; no one is left outside the all-encompassing love of Christ, and all have access to it by faith. As indicated in 3:12, the throne of grace is approachable to all through Christ.

Paul's Prayer (3:16–19)

Verses 3:16–19 follow a particular structure organized around three clauses, which begin with *hina* ("that"), three main verbs, and two pairs of aorist infinitives. Paul prays that God will *grant* certain things to the Ephesians and that the Ephesians will *be strong* and *be filled*. The flow of his prayer is that God would grant them strength through his Spirit and that Christ would dwell in them, and that the Ephesians would be strong both in understanding and in knowing, which can be summed up as being filled with or into God's fullness.

The first section of this prayer (3:16–18) addresses God as the one who fulfills or grants this prayer. Paul establishes that God is able from his abundant riches to grant these requests; this prayer is not one of desperation wherein the petitioner has little hope of getting a positive response. Indeed, Paul is confident that because of God's working through Christ, his prayer has every chance of success. Paul focuses on asking that the Ephesians be strengthened in power in their inner person. Paul is not speaking dualistically here, as though the body counts for nothing, and all that matters is the soul. The inner person is that which has been made new, and will receive a resurrected body. The inner person is the new creature in Christ, the member of Christ's body, the co-heir with God's household. Paul continues that this inner person is the home wherein Christ dwells by faith. Love has taken root and has established itself in each believer, making the indwelling of Christ something each believer can experience.

In 3:16, Paul asks that God act based on the wealth of his glory. Above in 3:13, Paul notes that his afflictions are the glory of the Ephesians; this glory is tied to the Ephesians being in Christ. In 3:16, Paul uses the term as that which defines and reflects God's character. God's glory, his character, his truth, is such that he is able to grant Paul's following requests for strength through the Spirit and the indwelling of Christ. Paul introduces with the phrase "strengthen you with power" the theme of power, which will carry through this prayer and doxology. The term for "power" carries the sense of ability or capability for action. This powerful strength is made available through the Spirit to work in the inner person. Paul uses this phrase "inner being" for several reasons. First, the terms for strength can be understood in a physical sense, such as being strong for battle. But Paul is speaking of the strength of character that informs the actions and attitudes of believers. Second, Paul focuses on the renewed self, that which is being transformed daily (2 Cor 4:16). Paul has in mind that aspect of the person that is attuned to God (Rom 7:22). The flesh, that which is part of this present age, will fade away. The new self, the inner person, however, is being transformed by the reality of new life in Christ. Third, Paul is not indicating with this phrase that a believer's faith is private. The inner person strengthened by God's Spirit is a different social, communal, public person—as Paul will outline in chs. 4–6. Finally, Paul drives home the point that the Christian life is powered by the Spirit. Today we might say that Christians run on electricity, not on batteries. God has not designed a motor that once he turns it on will run on its own. Instead, it needs a constant current, which is the Spirit.

Not only does Paul ask that they be strengthened, but also that they might have Christ dwell in their hearts through faith (3:17). It is possible that Paul suggests here that the strengthening of the inner person will lead to Christ taking up habitation in believers' hearts. But more likely Paul is paralleling this phrase with his request that through the Spirit the believers will be strong. As we have seen in several places in Ephesians thus far (1:12–13; 2:16–18; see also 4:3–6), Paul presents a vision of the Trinity, in this case working actively within believers that they might experience the fullness of God. In the final clause of this verse, Paul states that the believers have been established in love, a phrase that both glances back and looks forward in the prayer. This passage bridges his comment that Christ dwells in their hearts, for they have been rooted in love from the moment they were in Christ. But it also looks forward by offering a firm foundation, namely love, from which knowledge is possible.

Verses 3:18–19 include Paul's requests that the Ephesians might have the strength and the knowledge to see the universe as it really is and know Christ's love. Paul turns his attention to describing how his previous request, that God grant them strength and Christ's indwelling, will impact the Ephesians. He prays that they will be, by God's grace, supernaturally strong in their minds and hearts to comprehend the spiritual realities of God's love, power, and grace. Paul uses words of measurement—deep, wide, high, and long—but does not indicate what he is describing. This has led to several theories. Jerome and Augustine argue that Paul is describing the cross.[8] This idea has much to commend itself, including its

---

8. Jerome *Comm. Eph.* 3:16–19 (PL 26:491); Augustine *Ep.* 55.14.25 (PL 33:216).

vividness and creativity and its consistency with Paul's teaching that the cross is efficacious across the globe and through time. Another church father, John Chrysostom,[9] suggests God's love is in view, while Aquinas[10] argues it is Christ's love. Given Paul's insistence on both the Father's love and the Lord's love, these theories are strong as well. Paul has also stressed God's wisdom, made known in his salvation plan in Christ (3:10–11). Perhaps Paul's intention was to leave it deliberately vague, and thus inclusive of both love and wisdom, symbolized in the cross. Paul is asking that the believers appreciate the vastness of God's influence and control over the created order. "We thus should understand grasping the four dimensions as an invitation to grasp reality fully."[11]

Paul continues that this understanding is comprehensible only through the love of Christ, which surpasses all human knowledge. All this is possible because God's love and power is beyond anything we imagine, and because that power is active within us through Christ. If we had only knowledge of God's vastness, it would overwhelm our human frailty. But Paul anticipates this, and sandwiches his request for understanding between two pronouncements that love grounds and governs everything, including knowledge. It is not simply that God is greater than anything we can imagine, but that this great God is *for us*.

At the end of 3:19 we find our final *hina* clause, which signals the purpose behind Paul's beseeching: that the Ephesians might be filled with (or to) the fullness of God. Earlier in 1:23, using the same verb and noun, Paul explained that the church is Christ's body, which holds the fullness of Christ, who is filled with God's fullness entirely. In ch. 1, the context was Paul's thanksgiving and prayers that the Ephesians would perceive the hope of their calling, the wealth of their inheritance, and the great power of the one who works out our salvation (1:18–19). His prayer in 3:19 is similar, that they might be saturated with God's completeness and abundance, much like a sponge that can hold no more water.

The preposition used by Paul (*eis*) can be translated "with" or "into." In the first reading, the sense is that believers will be filled up with God's fullness; in the second, that believers will be filled to (into, towards) God's fullness. The second sense captures the idea of maturity and growth, that

9. John Chrysostom *Hom. Eph.* 3:18–19 (PG 62:51).

10. Thomas Aquinas, *Comm. Eph.*, ch. 3, lec 5 (vv. 18–21).

11. Neufeld 2002: 161.

the church as the body of Christ is daily growing towards God's fullness. The implications of this translation include a more robust appreciation for the presence of God in the congregation's midst. The point is not that believers become little gods but that the church as Christ's body has the capability to witness to the powers that exalt sin and its attending death. For the church to carry out its tasks in the world and make known God's wisdom to the rulers and authorities in the heavenlies or heavenly realms (3:9–10), a filling of God is essential. Again, God's fullness is not experienced as when we feel satiated after a big meal, for that sort of fullness makes us lethargic. Instead this is the fullness of the gas tank before the long drive. To continue the analogy, the journey involves the church being Christ to the world, and the destination is the new heavens and new earth, the great feast that awaits the redeemed.

Doxology (3:20–21)

The doxology is a fitting end to the section on theology and a poignant beginning to the discussion on ethics. Our neat categories, however, might not have been embraced by Paul. Could it be that he saw chs. 4–6 as outlining ways to worship? That the strength empowering the church in their daily activities was a form of worship? Perhaps specific words of praise are not the only means of worship, but worship might include each act consecrated by the indwelling Christ and the Spirit's power. Paul sets the tone for obedience—it comes from the church's new vision of reality—the unsurpassed love and wisdom of God the Trinity. From this place of awe and with the power given through the Spirit, the obedient walk of faith can be a joyful journey of worship.

The doxology highlights themes found throughout Ephesians, including God's power in creation, in the church, and in Christ. In 3:20 Paul twice uses terms rooted in "power" emphasizing God's capability to do what Paul has requested. Indeed, Paul recognizes that his requests merely scratch the surface of God's power to realize his wisdom and will over his creation. This power works in us, the church. The plural used here reflects Paul's conviction that God chooses to work through his people. God's glory is to be known and praised in the church and in Christ. God's glory is reflected in Christ, as the fullness of God dwells in Christ (Col 1:19). And since the church is Christ's body (1:22–23), it too reflects God's glory, in a secondary way. Paul's prayer and doxology share similar themes with

Jesus' prayer in John 17:1–26, including an emphasis on power, glory, knowledge, love, and the important role of the church. Both are permeated with a profound concern for the church. One might say that Eph 3:16–21 is Paul's high priestly prayer for the church.

EPHESIANS 4

Paul's detailed, robust theology and his personal witness to which the reader has been treated in the last three chapters has been leading up to his call in 4:1—to walk worthy of who you are in Christ. Carefully articulated theology must at some point be applied, and it is to this job that Paul now turns. The ethics enjoined upon believers is in keeping with the theological claims of the earlier chapters, and so we are not surprised to read about walking rightly and keeping unity and above all demonstrating love, for these traits are characteristic of the Godhead whom believers serve. The goal of good theology, then, is an upright life, moving to maturity, able to discern spiritual matters and understand God's wisdom. Paul asks the Ephesians twice to walk in a particular manner (4:1, 17). These calls serve to organize the chapter into halves, the first dealing with the one God giving specific gifts for the one body (church), and the second looking at the new person renewed by the Spirit to be one with other members of the body. In the chapter, Paul's burden is to encourage believers in a holy lifestyle based on key theological truths. First, the God who calls is the one God; hence the believers ought also to live in unity. Second, the Christ who calls has the full measure of grace for each believer, and from that grace gives gifts to spur on wisdom and growth.

ONE BODY IN CHRIST, DIVERSE GIFTS (4:1–16)

¹As a prisoner for the Lord, then, I urge you to live a life worthy of the calling you have received. ²Be completely humble and gentle; be patient, bearing with one another in love. ³Make every effort to keep the unity of the Spirit through the bond of peace. ⁴There is one body and one Spirit, just as you were called to one hope when you were called; ⁵one Lord, one faith, one baptism; ⁶one God and Father of all, who is over all

and through all and in all. [7]But to each one of us grace has been given as Christ apportioned it. [8]This is why it says:

> "When he ascended on high,
> he took many captives
> and gave gifts to his people."

[9](What does "he ascended" mean except that he also descended to the lower, earthly regions? [10]He who descended is the very one who ascended higher than all the heavens, in order to fill the whole universe.) [11]So Christ himself gave the apostles, the prophets, the evangelists, the pastors and teachers, [12]to equip his people for works of service, so that the body of Christ may be built up [13]until we all reach unity in the faith and in the knowledge of the Son of God and become mature, attaining to the whole measure of the fullness of Christ. [14]Then we will no longer be infants, tossed back and forth by the waves, and blown here and there by every wind of teaching and by the cunning and craftiness of people in their deceitful scheming. [15]Instead, speaking the truth in love, we will in all things grow up into him who is the head, that is, Christ. [16]From him the whole body, joined and held together by every supporting ligament, grows and builds itself up in love, as each part does its work.

Christians rightly stress the importance of understanding God's work in Christ, and the centuries of creedal formation attest to the critical nature of getting theology correct. Far too often, however, believers stop at that point, resting complacently in their (false) assumption that to know the right answer is to be right with God. Paul's injunctions to the Ephesians suggests otherwise. Right theology leads to right living; indeed the two are not easily compartmentalized, as Paul's comments attest. His argument begins with a call to walk uprightly, but quickly grows to include a declaration of God's oneness and the church's one calling. Theological truths support ethical behavior: to have the former without the latter is the height of arrogance, and to have the latter without the former is hollow legalism. The structure of his argument flows from a call to walk in a manner consistent with their calling as believers (4:1–6), followed by two additional notes. First, that each believer is given grace by Christ, who also gives to his body gifts of theological leadership in the form of apostles, prophets, evangelists, shepherds, and teachers (4:7–12). Second, each person being thus equipped for ministry will grow into Christ (4:13–16).

One Calling by the One God (4:1–6)

In this single sentence in Greek, Paul exhorts his readers to grab hold of, in an experiential way, the unique standing they enjoy in Christ. Paul uses the indicative form of *parakaleō* (to encourage or exhort) here and in a similar phrase in Rom 12:1. In both places, the exhortation to holy living follows immediately after a doxology. The vision of the exalted God leads Paul to urge believers fervently to act in such a way that their lives testify to the truth of that awe-inspiring vision. Paul stresses several key terms that will guide his argument throughout the chapter: calling, love, and unity. And he imagines this unity in love being realized in the daily lives of believers. Paul speaks of walking one's calling, of having humility and meekness which models the character of the Triune God and reflects the hope of our salvation. His status as prisoner in the Lord operates in the background and will serve as an example of leadership when he speaks of gifts in 4:11.

Paul's metaphorical use of the term "walk" (translated in TNIV as "live a life") reveals his deep Jewish heritage. Often Jewish writers speak of a faithful life as walking with God. The image creates a picture of action, effort, and purpose. Paul uses the verb elsewhere (5:2, 8, 15) as he envisions the believers' faithful, fruitful lives in Christ. He also uses the word once (2:2) to reference the habits and lifestyle the Ephesians previously engaged in prior to their calling. Paul strongly urges the Thessalonians to walk worthy of their calling in God's Kingdom (1 Thess 2:11–12; see also Phil 1:27; Col 1:10). In describing this life, Paul does not offer here a list of dos and don'ts, but sets before them holy attitudes that should govern all actions. Paul highlights three: humility, gentleness, and patience. Interestingly, in his speech to the Ephesians in Acts 20:19, Paul uses the same rare term for humility that we find here. In this speech, he points to his own actions among the Ephesians, how he served the Lord by courageously preaching the good news in the teeth of tough opposition. Paul is speaking to them on his journey to Jerusalem, expecting that hardships, imprisonments, and afflictions await him (he was correct). He encourages them to help the weak, and quotes a saying of Jesus not in our gospels that it is more blessed to give than to receive (Acts 20:35).

Fusing the Horizons: Paul's Sermons and Letters

Paul's farewell address to the Ephesians in Acts 20:18–35 gets scant attention in commentaries on Ephesians, in large part because the epistle's Pauline authorship is questioned. Even if Pauline authorship is granted, the second hurdle is Luke's reliability in presenting Paul's speech. We have already dealt with the authorship question extensively in the Introduction. Some call into question the authenticity of Luke's rendering of Paul's speech, but in favor of its reliability is its placement in Miletus, not Ephesus. This relatively insignificant venue supports the speech's historicity. Others argue that Luke is a trustworthy preserver of Paul's essential message, even if the wording is Lukan, by pointing to the topics in this speech and similar themes found within Paul's epistles. For example, these terms are used in both: "gospel," "grace," as well as the phrase "faith in our Lord Jesus Christ." Paul emphasizes that he spoke to both Jews and Gentiles (Acts 20:21) and that he faced trials in Ephesus (see also 1 Cor 15:32). Both in Acts 20:28 and in Eph 1:7, he emphasizes the blood of Christ which brings forgiveness of sins; additionally, he speaks of the building up of the body (Eph 2:20–22; Acts 20:32). He notes that he worked hard among them, not taking any free handouts. This information was not part of Luke's account of Paul's journeys, but is scattered throughout Paul's letters (1 Thess 2:9; 1 Cor 9:12); in Eph 4:28 he encourages them not to steal, but to work hard that they might be able to take care of needs in their midst. Again, Paul stresses that the Ephesians have an inheritance because they are sanctified (Eph 1:18, Acts 20:32). What we find in Paul's farewell address to the Ephesians is consistent with his letter to them. In both Paul exhorts them to remain steadfast, reminds them of his own work among them, reiterates to them that they (Jew and Gentile) share an inheritance in Christ, and encourages them in the building up of the body of Christ.

It is not by accident that Paul connects in his mind Jesus' teachings and the term humility, for this characteristic is distinctive of Christianity, not the Gentile Roman world of Ephesus. Indeed, well-known philosophers such as Epictetus (50–130 CE) disparage humility as dishonorable for a free person to display, for it debases them in the eyes of their peers.[1] Yet according to Paul, humility is an appropriate posture for believers, because they do not compare themselves to others but see themselves as servants of God.

Gentleness is the second attitude noted by Paul; Jesus is described as gentle of heart (Matt 11:29), and Paul uses both humility and gentleness in describing Christ (2 Cor 10:1). In Gal 5:23, the characteristic is among the fruit of the Spirit. Gentleness was viewed more positively by the wider Roman world. The term carried the sense of the middle ground between constant anger at everyone and no anger at all. It also had the sense of a trainer taming a wild horse. In any case, it does not have the sense of being weak in the face of struggle or lacking courage. Finally, Paul speaks of patience (see also a list of the fruit of the Spirit in Gal 5:22). Together these character traits can be thought of as the necessary traveler's kit for all believers as they embark on their journey of faith. To be faithful to their calling, to express Christian love, to model unity requires the supernatural grace offered by God in Christ through the Spirit, witnessed by the one baptism and one faith shared by all believers.

The oneness in love that should characterize the church is rooted in the gospel claims about the God who calls (see also 1 Cor 1:26). In 1:18, Paul speaks of the hope of our calling that believers might ever more deeply understand and appreciate the riches of God's salvation. The hope of the calling is that all things will be summed up in Christ (1:10), including overcoming both humanity's estrangement from God and creation's decay. It is through the invitation that God calls, and his call reflects his purposes in his redemption plan (Rom 9:11). A foretaste of that hope fully realized is the unity between Jew and Gentile in the church. If you need proof that our resurrection hope will be actualized fully in God's time, just look at the church, created through the death and resurrection of Christ and united in Christ through the Spirit. While we don't always see this unity within our churches today, the fact of the matter is that the power that raised Jesus is the same power that made Gentiles members of God's family. Christ *is* our peace, and Paul suggests that one sure way to

---

1. Epictetus *Diatr.* 3.24.56.

confirm our resurrection hope that all will be made new is to reflect on the reality of Christ's body, the church.

In 4:1, 4, Paul describes God's call having a calling on the Ephesians' lives. In classical Greek, calling meant a summons to court or an invitation to a feast. So we might rephrase Paul here to say that God summons with a summons or God invites with a particular message of invitation, namely the gospel message of Jesus Christ. Paul uses the term calling in 1 Cor 7:20, where Paul exhorts the Corinthians not to seek to change their social status after they were called by God, for whether or not one was a slave when called, in the Lord all are free. Likewise in Phil 3:14 we have a sense of invitation, wherein Paul speaks of forgetting what is past and straining towards the future, the upward call of God. Further understanding of calling is found in Rom 11:29, "for God's gift and his call are irrevocable." The context is the oneness of Jew and Gentile in Christ and the conviction that God has not abandoned his people, but has enlarged their numbers (by including Gentiles) through Christ.

In 4:4–6, Paul explains why unity and oneness are critical to the church's witness by listing seven "ones" that form the basis for the church's oneness in Spirit. Paul expresses a similar thought in 1 Cor 8:6, wherein he contrasts the pagan acceptance of many gods and the Christian (and Jewish) steadfast stand on monotheism. Thus when the church lacks unity, it calls into question its proclamation of the oneness of God. The oneness of God is not an intellectual belief only. James 2:19 warns that even the demons believe God is one, and they shudder. The unity or oneness is of a certain type, namely Trinitarian. Without putting too fine a point on it, the three Persons in one Godhead provides a picture of the oneness of the diverse elements in the church—Jew, Gentile; slave, free; male, female.

The Gift to Grow On (4:7–16)

Paul begins a new thought with the qualifier "but" (*de*) as he digs deeper into the subject of unity. Though there is one call to be the one body of Christ in one faith and baptism, the individual believer is not lost in some sort of great collective. Each believer is given grace by Christ, who, having both descended and ascended, has the authority to give gifts. Paul expounds what was given, why it was given, how long the gifts are to be in effect, and then returns to explain from another angle why his gifts are so crucial to the church. The themes of unity, love, and Christian maturity permeate this passage. The images are full of motion as Paul presents the ignorant as thrown about by winds and waves, and the wise as standing fast against the gale. Verse 16 circles back to v. 7 by concluding that each member grows in love and together with other members makes up the maturing body of Christ.

In 4:7 Paul speaks of *the* grace given to each of us according to the measure of Christ's gift ("the" is not translated in the TNIV). This verse has given rise to several interpretations, in part because certain terms, including measure, grace, and gift, carry a range of meaning. Before exploring possible meanings of these terms, we should note what the statement does not imply. Paul is not claiming that God gives more salvation grace to some than to others, or that he limits his grace to some but not to others. Jerome uses an interesting analogy.[2] He likens the grace of God to the waters of the sea, which to humans appear infinite. Picture a scene wherein a person stood knee deep in the ocean, and many came to him with vessels to be filled with seawater. He could only give as much seawater as those individuals could hold, while all around them the sea waves lapped. The supply was endless, but the vessels were finite. So too, the grace of Christ is infinite, and is poured into finite humans. Nor does the phrase imply that some believers have more grace to live their daily lives than do others. Christ's grace is unfathomable.

Returning to contested terms, dictionary definitions of *metron* or "apportionment" include (a) a standard, rule, or means of measurement, (b) a certain portion in contrast to another amount, and (c) quantity, size, or length. The various interpretations of "measure" are not given in isolation of decisions about the meaning of grace and gift in 4:7. Often the gift noted in 4:7 is related to the list of leaders in 4:11. The argument contends that the gift given by Christ is the special levels of grace or the abilities that include apostles, prophets, and so on. Thus the phrase "according to the measure of the gift of Christ" means that each believer gets a gift and Christ determines the amount of the gift. However, the focus in 4:11 is not on giving gifts to particular people, but Christ out of his abundance granting aid to the church. I will say more about this below; here let me note a few points. First, the term "gift" is singular in 4:7, while the listing of that which Christ gives in 4:11 contains several items. Second, Paul includes himself in 4:7 when he says "to each *of us*." This suggests one

---

2. Jerome *Comm. Eph.*; translation in Heine 2002: 171.

of two things: either Paul had in mind *only* leaders of the church when he spoke of the grace and gift given, or he intended to include everyone as receiving the grace. I think the latter is more likely, especially because Paul does not identify himself as an apostle in this chapter, but as a prisoner in the Lord.

Finally, the argument that Paul speaks in 4:7 about gifts often treats grace and gift (understood as a plural) as synonyms. A possible subtext of this interpretive move is that while Christ gives grace to everyone, he gives a bit more to some, and we call them apostles, evangelists, and pastors. This argument equates Paul's phrase about the measure of the gift with a variety of gifts, something Paul does not state here. Paul does not use the term "gifts" (*charismata*) in either 4:7 or 4:11, as he does in 1 Cor 12:4 or Rom 12:6. In 1 Cor 12:11, however, Paul does describe different gifts as coming from the one Spirit, different ministries from the one Lord, and different activities being worked out by the same God. But in Eph 4:7, Paul's point centers on unity, not different gifts. Each of us, Paul declares, has grace, because Christ defeated captivity and as victor, can give gifts (plural in the quotation) to his people (4:8–10).

The Romans passage is more difficult to interpret. In Rom 12:6, Paul speaks of different gifts being given according to the grace, and in 12:3 speaks about the "measure of faith." He begins his argument in 12:3 by cautioning that each believer should think soberly about themselves, adding that God has apportioned a measure of faith to each. At a glance this text might seem parallel to our Ephesians text, so a careful read is in order. First we ask why people might be tempted to think more highly of themselves. Did they think that they possessed more virtue or talent or gifting from God? Paul is presumably countering the Romans' view that some believers have more of something than do others. Thus the term "measure" here probably should be understood as a means or standard of measurement. Additionally, often the phrase "of faith" is understood as a partitive genitive, suggesting that Paul is stressing either a special miracle-working faith or an individual Christian's personal faith response to God. Paul would be saying that some Christians received more of faith (of some kind) than did others.

This interpretation, however, does not fit with Paul's claim that they not think more highly of themselves, for if indeed someone did have more faith, it makes sense that they value that more highly than someone who is lacking faith. A better interpretation would be to understand measure as standard and the genitive as one of apposition. In this case, Paul would be arguing that believers should measure themselves against the standard of the faith, the gospel message, with the implication that since all are saved only by God's grace, no believer has reason to think more highly of herself.[3] This faith, this gospel, is the standard by which we should judge ourselves. Following this reasoning, Paul takes a turn in Rom 12:6, wherein he introduces the term "different," which modifies "gifts" (*charismata*), not "grace." The point is that believers have different gifts, but they all spring from the same grace of 12:3. In sum, grace is the unifying point and the faith is the standard raised in 12:3, from which different gifts spring forth for the edification of the body of Christ.[4]

Returning to Ephesians, Paul stresses in 4:7 the unity of the body; he is not speaking about differences of gifts, as he does in 1 Corinthians and Rom 12:6 noted above. Instead, Paul continues his discussion of the one church, in which all believers have the same grace in the same measure. The result is that we all as the body receive the gift of Christ, which enables the body to grow. As we will see below in 4:11, Paul does not address different gifts; rather he indicates that the church receives aid for its ministry in the form of apostles, prophets, and so on. To anticipate our conclusion in 4:11, the gift is a collection of tools and resources that outfit believers to do ministry; those resources are called apostles, pastors, etc. To walk worthy of our calling, we need wisdom and training in discernment, which comes through prophets, evangelists, and teachers. Paul's thought flow continues with the theme of unity from 4:4 through 4:13. Diversity, a key term in today's discussions, reveals itself in the saints' ministry, wherein each member of the church works faithfully to build up the body of Christ. Tolerance is another popular term today, but not one I'd venture to say Paul would have accepted because for him the major goal of each believer is not self-fulfillment but being a growing member of a strong, loving church.

3. Cranfield 1979: 613–16; Fitzmyer 1993: 645–46. For an opposing position, see Dunn 1988: 721–28.

4. Keener (2009: 145–46) holds that Rom 12:3–6 indicates God gives different faith apportionments (not amounts) as pertains to the gifts given. This view highlights the similar phrases "*metron* of faith" in 12:3 and "*analogian* of faith" in 12:6. The conclusion drawn is that the latter should not be translated as "standard of faith" as if in 12:6 Paul limits the "*analogian* of faith" to the gift of prophecy, whereas in fact Paul believes that God provides the kind of faith that energizes each kind of gift.

Paul defends his claim in 4:7 that Christ gives grace by citing Ps 68:18, which includes an interesting phrase "he took many captives" or "taking captivity captive." Christ takes captive through his death and resurrection the powers of this present age of captivity to evil and death. The ironic corollary is that Christ can be said to defeat all captivities. In this freedom from captivity, Christ has the power to bestow gifts. Such language brings to mind both Paul's own chains, and also the captivity that Gentiles long suffered. Paul knew that his own prison chains were but confirmation of his apostleship to the Gentiles, who now enjoy the full measure of God's grace through Christ. In quoting a few lines from this psalm, Paul points to the entire song of praise celebrating God's great victory over evil and Israel's enemies. Interestingly, in Hebrew the verse quoted by Paul reads, "and he *received* gifts from men." The Greek text, from which Paul quotes, reads "and he *gave* gifts to people." The change is likely due to a reversal of two Hebrew letters in the verb, but Jerome[5] suggests that because the psalmist looked forward to the day when Christ would be victorious, he used the word "received," but Paul could now use the term "gave" because Christ's redemptive work on the cross is finished. Moreover, it was typical in Paul's day for the victorious general, after he collected all the plunder, to distribute it among his faithful soldiers.

While the psalm focuses on the ascent, marking God's victory, Paul elaborates that the ascent necessarily implies a descent. Most see an allusion to the incarnation, and his ascent a reference to his resurrection and victory over sin and death, which awaits final consummation. Because he is over all things, he has the authority and right to grant gifts. A similar claim is made in 1:23; here Paul explains that Christ is filled with God's fullness, and Christ fills the church with that fullness.

It is out of this fullness that apostles, prophets, evangelists, pastors, and teachers are given. Right away we are confronted with two problems. First, the Greek literally reads, "he gave some apostles, some prophets," and so on. Often translators insert a "to be" verb, so that the verse would read "he gave some to be apostles" or "the gifts he gave were that some would be apostles." This is certainly possible, given that in Greek one need not include the verb "to be" in every situation. But did Paul expect his readers to insert the verb here? If we answer yes, then we likely see 4:7 as anticipating the giving of different gifts. As noted above, this seems a less

5. Jerome *Comm. Eph*; translation in Heine 2002: 172.

persuasive approach. A negative response to the question looks forward to 4:12, suggesting that Paul's point is that Christ gives particular aids to the church, so that the saints can do the ministry to which they are called. It is crucial to note that what Christ gives, he gives to the church. We might imagine Christ handing out a gift box to his body, containing the vitamins it needs to grow strong. The focus is on saints equipped for ministry and church growth, not on individuals receiving special gifting. The advantage of this appraisal is that it is a more straightforward read of the Greek.

Second, 4:12 lists three prepositional phrases, and their relationship to each other, as well as to the preceding verse, has given rise to two competing interpretations. The phrases in Greek are "for [*pros*] the equipping of the saints," "to [*eis*] the work of ministry," and "to [*eis*] the building of the body of Christ." For two main reasons, one position understands the first clause as primary, and the second clause in a subordinate position (see the TNIV translation above). First, the different prepositions signal that the clauses are not of equal weight. Second, Paul uses a noun (*katartismos*) in the first clause that is not found elsewhere in the New Testament, but whose cognate verb occurs frequently and is translated as "equipping" or "perfecting." Choosing the first option, the phrase would read "equipping the saints," which raises the question: equipping them for what? The answer, indicated by the preposition *eis*, is for the work of the ministry. This position argues that the gift given to the church is for the saints to be equipped to do their ministry, which is to build up the church. The saints are equipped in their tasks by the gift, namely the apostles, prophets, evangelists, shepherds, and teachers who instruct the saints and nurture the body of Christ. This argument fits well not only in accounting for the different prepositions, but also with Paul's overarching emphasis that the gift and Christ's riches are given to every member of Christ's body (Eph 1:3–19; 3:20).

The second position argues that each of the prepositional phrases is independent of the other two, and all three refer back to the responsibilities and activities of the apostles, prophets, evangelists, pastors, and teachers. In this interpretation, the noun *katartismos* is translated as "perfecting" or "training" the saints. "The primary context here in v. 12 is the function and role of Christ's specific gifts, the ministers, not that of all the saints."[6] Although this position rightly notes that the prepositional change is not on its own indicative of a connection between the first and second clauses, the argument fails to account for adequately Paul's general emphasis in the passage, namely the activity of the saints. Paul refers to them at the beginning of 4:12, not at the end,[7] where one might expect them to be mentioned if Paul was focused on the ministers as this second argument contends. In sum, Paul's message about Christ's gift to the church is that the ministers might serve the saints so that the saints might be well prepared to do the work of ministry. The goal for each group is a stronger, healthier body of Christ.

Interestingly, Paul does not mention his own apostleship in this discussion. In fact, except for the opening line of the epistle, he speaks of himself not as an apostle but as a prisoner of Christ or an ambassador in chains. Since he is not shy about discussing his apostleship to the Galatians or Corinthians, for example (1 Cor 4:9–16; 2 Cor 13:2–4, 10; Gal 1:1, 11), we might wonder why the image of prisoner is front and center here. He uses a term that conjures up the picture of someone in chains (4:1), and then using a cognate term, speaks of the believers being bound together (4:3). The word picture is interesting: I am a prisoner, and you should be prisoners of each other. If Paul had called attention to his own apostleship, that would shift the focus to diverse *charismata* (as in Rom 12:4–8 and 1 Cor 12:4–13) rather than the gift of grace, maintaining unity, which is extended to each believer.

Fusing the Horizons: Ministry and the Church

In 4:12, Paul explains the reason for Christ's gift, that the saints would be equipped to do the work of ministry. Today we tend to think of pastors as those in the ministry, but Paul turns that picture on its head. It is the saints, each and every believer, who do the ministry of the church. The gift Christ extends, which is comprised of those who explain the gospel, serves to strengthen that ministry. So often we think of church leadership and ministry as synonyms, but actually the former is only a single aspect of the latter. Neufeld offers a

6. Lincoln 1990: 253.

7. O'Brien 1999: 302–5. He writes on 305, "The exalted Messiah gives ministries of the word to equip God's people for work in his service so as to build his body."

useful analogy of player-coach to describe Paul's point.[8] The player-coach is also part of the team which takes the playing field; he or she is a single element of the team's success (or failure). Paul is not concerned here to speak about individual gifts (*charismata*) but about the outcome of those gifts on the saints. He is interested in describing what a body that has been "apostle-ized," "prophet-ized," "evangelized," "pastor-ized," and "teacher-ized" looks like. The focus is not on those using particular gifts, but the effect of those gifts on the body. This could be a refreshing way to look at our own church structures, which tend to isolate ministry in the hands of paid staff. And it fits tightly with the picture of the church drawn thus far in Ephesians: a church unified through Christ, sealed with the Spirit, witnessing to the world God's redemption by showing peace to all for all are God's children, and balancing that with a strong grip on truth, letting God's light shine forth unapologetically in love.

The saints are equipped not only for the work of ministry but to build up the body (4:12, 16). This theme is not new to the letter, for we see it stressed in 2:20–21, which focuses on the church comprised of both Jews and Gentiles being built upon the foundation of the apostles and prophets. Additionally, both 4:16 and 2:21 speak of the body being fitted together, thereby reinforcing Paul's central theme of unity. Within the entire letter, such oneness is primarily understood as the union in Christ of Jew and Gentile. Although in this section Paul does not explicitly mention Jew and Gentile, it is likely in his mind, for he references Gentiles in 2:17 when he contrasts the Ephesians' old way of life as Gentiles with their new life in Christ.

One final point must be made concerning 4:12. Paul states that the saints are equipped for the *work* of ministry, the up-building of the body of Christ. In 2:10, Paul declares that God has prepared in advance good works for believers. Are these good works the same as the work of ministry? If so, then the picture of the good works is a corporate one wherein each member of the church participates in the overall good work of the church in building up the body of Christ in unity and fullness of knowledge. This perspective is a helpful corrective to our Western individualism, which tends to see 2:10 as speaking about individual acts of piety.

8. Neufeld 2002: 196.

More likely Paul has in mind the corporate witness of the church in the world to be the body of Christ, unified in Him.

In 4:13–16, Paul creates a vivid picture contrasting an infant and an adult. The former is unstable and vulnerable to every dishonorable, deceitful person seeking an advantage. But the mature are stable because they are grounded in the truth; they have reached the standard or measure of Christ's fullness. The choice of verb is interesting. Paul speaks of our *arriving* at this mature adult and fullness status, implying a lifelong journey. The goal is a fully formed and functioning body of Christ with each part contributing to the health of the whole. In this description Paul tracks a middle path between two common extremes. First, Paul underscores the importance of correct doctrine, both in his insistence on having a proper knowledge of the gospel's teachings and in his compelling picture of the immature believer tossed like a rag doll on the winds of every passing doctrinal fad. Often today Christians downplay doctrine as a way to bring unity, but ecumenism gained by such a method is illusory. Paul emphasizes truth *in love*, which implies a humble spirit straining after Christ. Second, Paul cannot imagine a godly knowledge without practical witness. Teaching the truth in love is a means to the goal of equipping saints for ministry. Truth is to be lived out in such a way that the body of Christ grows bigger as new members are added and each one gains maturity; grows stronger as each by themselves and together understand more fully the riches of Christ; and grows steadier as the church stands firm in the face of struggles.

Fusing the Horizons: Refusing to Walk the Walk—So What?

The gift of Christ (4:11) speaks to the theological needs of the congregation. For Paul, right belief leads to right behavior. Right behavior done repeatedly leads to strong unified churches wherein all members develop in their roles in the body. But what if one behaves badly, or discounts the importance of unity and peace? What are the ramifications if we do not walk as befits our calling? Paul indicates that we are then no better than toddlers at the mercy of devious people (4:14). We are destined to behave in lewd ways, with darkened minds (4:17–18). Some today suggest that Paul was not strong enough in his condemnation of bad behavior, but this fails to appreciate the historical context. In the first century CE, to be condemned to ignorance was a terrible and shameful fate. When someone decided to join a philosophical group, such as follow a Stoic, Epicurean, or Cynic teacher, they expected to be taught both how to think and how to act. The ancient world assumed this connection and so any person interested in the virtuous life would look to the philosophers' teachings, expecting that with their new knowledge they would also modify their lifestyle. A similar expectation would be present with the gospel message; believers would assume that correct teachings would lead to proper actions. Today, however, some wonder why Paul does not threaten the Ephesians with punishment if they refuse to follow his directives on right behavior. But Paul does not need to cry out hellfire and brimstone if his fellow believers don't change their ways, for he (and they) assume that they joined the church in part to learn how to live differently. They would expect to be asked to change behaviors, even as they would expect to learn different ideas. Because today's church can so narrowly define salvation as having the right answers, it ends up separating what for Paul is an organic whole, thought and deed.

WALK IN NEW LIFE (EPH 4:17–32)

[17]So I tell you this, and insist on it in the Lord, that you must no longer live as the Gentiles do, in the futility of their thinking. [18]They are darkened in their understanding and separated from the life of God because of the ignorance that is in them due to the hardening of their hearts. [19]Having lost all sensitivity, they have given themselves over to sensuality so as to indulge in every kind of impurity, and they are full of greed. [20]That, however, is not the way of life you learned [21]when you heard about Christ and were taught in him in accordance with the truth that is in Jesus. [22]You were taught, with regard to your former way of life, to put off your old self, which is being corrupted by its deceitful desires; [23]to be made new in the attitude of your minds; [24]and to put on the new self, created to be like God in true righteousness and holiness. [25]Therefore each of you must put off falsehood and speak truthfully to your neighbor, for we are all members of

one body. [26]"In your anger do not sin": Do not let the sun go down while you are still angry, [27]and do not give the devil a foothold. [28]Those who have been stealing must steal no longer, but must work, doing something useful with their own hands, that they may have something to share with those in need. [29]Do not let any unwholesome talk come out of your mouths, but only what is helpful for building others up according to their needs, that it may benefit those who listen. [30]And do not grieve the Holy Spirit of God, with whom you were sealed for the day of redemption. [31]Get rid of all bitterness, rage and anger, brawling and slander, along with every form of malice. [32]Be kind and compassionate to one another, forgiving each other, just as in Christ God forgave you.

A second time in this chapter Paul entreats the Ephesians to walk in a particular way. In 4:1, it was to walk worthy of one's calling, and in 4:17 it is to walk in a manner completely opposite that of the Gentiles. The calling of God is antithetical to paganism because the latter is alienated from the one true God. A sharp contrast is drawn, on the one hand, between the Gentiles whose wisdom is futile and whose minds run to immorality and, on the other hand, the believers who know or learn Christ (4:20). This truth is lived out in great measure by their kind, compassionate speech which encourages others. The visual picture drawn in this section is the putting off of the old person, and the putting on of the new. Paul's anthropology and eschatology are revealed in this image of old and new, but the meaning of section 4:20–24 has been contested and so will be examined closely below. Before turning to examine this section in depth, a comment about Gentiles in this argument is in order. In Paul's larger world, people were divided into categories, including a fundamental one of Jew and Gentile. There was no third option. But for Paul, when a person is in Christ, they no longer fit the world's categories. They are not Jew, but they are also not Gentile. This completely new category only exists in the new age, which has broken in on the present age with Christ's resurrection. The revolutionary power of God can be seen in our midst with a completely new people created in Christ, and the church's ongoing witness is to live in line with this new reality.

Paul insists in 4:20–21 that the Ephesians learned Christ; they were taught truth in Jesus. He follows this statement with three infinitives which all relate back to the verb "were taught." The first and last infinitive, "to put off" and "to put on," are in the past (aorist) tense, while the second infinitive "to be made new" is in the present tense. The primary questions revolve around how to translate these infinitives, especially the first and last ones. Do they describe the result of the teaching? If so, then Paul would be emphasizing the previous facts that believers have shed their old self and put on their new self in Christ. Or do they indicate the purpose of the teaching? In this case, the infinitives would serve as imperatives encouraging believers to act by taking off the old person and putting on the new person. For answers to this dilemma, we look to other places in Paul's letters where he uses similar language. The closest parallel is Col 3:9–10, which includes the participles "put off" and "put on" in past tense, along with the present participle "made new" or "renewing." The new person is that wonderful creation in Christ which does not allow categorization by old ways—Jew, Gentile, slave, free, etc. All are in Christ (3:11). A second example is Rom 6:2–8, where Paul makes clear that in baptism the believer dies to his or her old self, and is raised to new life (see also Gal 3:27). The old self no longer has power because the old age to which it belongs is passing away. Thus believers need no longer heed its siren calls to sin, for even sin's power has been broken; believers are now slaves of righteousness. From these examples, many rightly conclude that Paul in Eph 4:20–24 intends that believers have shed their old self and put on their new self already, perhaps in their baptism.

However, Paul also uses the language of putting off and putting on in his injunctions to live a new life. In Rom 13:12, 14 Paul encourages the Romans to put on the armor of light. Additionally, in Eph 4:23 Paul speaks in the present tense of believers being renewed by the Spirit or spirit ("attitude" in TNIV) of their minds. This suggests a daily, ongoing commitment to act in a manner pleasing to God, which invites comment on Paul's view of human and divine agency. Christians down through the centuries have debated the interrelationship between divine and human agency. A question often asked is whether humans have free will to do God's will. Paul holds a strict dualism between light and darkness, truth and falsehood. He maintains that a person is either a slave of sin or a slave of righteousness (Rom 6:17–18). This division seems to run straight through a believer's heart inasmuch as the attraction to sin is still active, even though sin's power has been put to death on the cross. The gravitational pull of sin is greatly lessened if the believer is clothed in the new person who was created in the likeness of God (4:24). We have a saying that "the clothes make the man (or woman)" and a similar sentiment applies to believers, for in both cases the clothing affects the person's own mental picture of themselves. Isn't that why young children love to dress up as super heroes or knights or princesses—the feeling of power attached with their outfit? So too a believer who dresses themselves in Christ knows themselves to be different, changed, more fully equipped to do their ministry.

Yet, are they powered by their own energy? Or is divine agency present as well? Paul stresses God's role in revealing truth and generating wisdom and knowledge upon which believers can act. Moreover, Paul insists that believers do not simply know *about* Christ, but they learned Christ and were taught in him (4:20–21). Finally, Paul notes that the spirit of their minds is being renewed (4:23). In using the passive voice, most likely here Paul speaks of their spirit being renewed by the Holy Spirit. Paul once again emphasizes the inextricable connection between head and heart, between a renewed mind and a reformed lifestyle. Knowing *about* Christ keeps the Savior at a distance, but knowing Christ invites a radical reorganization of one's view of reality and priorities.

The promise in this section is that the believer is a new person (see also 2 Cor 5:17). The new person belongs to the new age; he or she is a citizen of heaven (Phil 3:20). She is destined for glory, and is now sealed with the Spirit for that Day. So far, I have painted a very individualistic picture, which is only half of the story for Paul. Paul speaks of believers growing mature, by which he means that they grow as a body into their head, Christ (4:15). Christians understand themselves not simply as one with God in Christ, but as one with other members of Christ's body. In Africa, there is a saying, "I am because we are." This proverb sums up well Paul's mindset concerning believers. A Christian is not merely one who is saved in Christ, but is one who simultaneously is a member with others in Christ's body, the church. One cannot be a body-less Christian, in Paul's imagination. For him, the reality of Christ's body, made up of this new person (neither Jew nor Gentile), speaks to the reality of each member's resurrection hope.

Paul gets practical in his advice in 4:25–32. Notice that the injunctions to godly behavior have to do with interpersonal relationships. Paul enjoins those who have put off falsehood to speak truth to their fellow Christ followers (4:25), which includes resisting anger, slander, and bitterness (4:31). James, in his letter, notes as well the power of the tongue to build up or destroy a community (Jas 3:6–12). Paul also warns strongly against allowing anger to fester (4:26). Sadly, many of us have been part of church fights that pit one group against another. Had the wounds been exposed to the healing air and cleansed carefully, the body would have healed in time. Paul is under no illusions that the devil has designs to weaken Christ's body, and one avenue of attack is through fomenting anger (4:27). Paul describes a personal situation wherein someone at Corinth had personally insulted him publicly. He asks that the Corinthians address firmly the slander, which apparently they did. Thus he cautions them that since the person did repent, the rest must receive him back with open arms and hearts, so that Satan will not gain the upper hand over the community (2 Cor 4:5–11).

In addition to watching their words closely, Paul suggests that the Ephesians work at their jobs in order to have enough to aid other members of Christ who have needs (4:28). Paul directs thieves to cease stealing, which may imply that some Ephesians were stealing. In Paul's day, slaves might take from their masters, or workers from their employers—the struggles of life can feel overwhelming and people choose what initially looks like the easy way out. But Paul charges them to toil at their work, not that they might get rich, but that they would have enough left over for those who because of illness or disability might be unable to work. The temptations to steal things or time from our employers remain strong today, but what seems quick and painless is really ultimately selfish, for a stolen good cannot be shared. Paul understands work as something that benefits the entire community, as those with jobs and income can provide goods, services, and money to those who lack the resources to make a living themselves. An example of such an attitude is the Macedonians, as Paul describes in 2 Cor 8:1–5. Paul celebrates these churches (including the Philippians, Thessalonians, and Bereans, for example) and their example of giving to the Judean churches in need. The Macedonians in their destitute poverty considered it supreme joy to give beyond what was thought possible, so that they might be part of God's activities in Judea. They understood that the (little) money they earned was not only for themselves, but could be used for kingdom purposes, building the body of Christ across the world. Their eyes were lifted beyond their own limited horizons of their household, to the broader vision of the church in their town and across the globe. In the next chapter, Paul continues to encourage the Ephesians with a vision for their life in Christ. He reminds them of who they are: beloved children of God and those loved by Christ. From that sure place, they can step out in love to others.

EPHESIANS 5

WALKING AS CHRIST WALKED (5:1–20)

¹Follow God's example, therefore, as dearly loved children ²and walk in the way of love, just as Christ loved us and gave himself up for us as a fragrant offering and sacrifice to God. ³But among you there must not be even a hint of sexual immorality, or of any kind of impurity, or of greed, because these are improper for the Lord's people. ⁴Nor should there be obscenity, foolish talk or coarse joking, which are out of place, but rather thanksgiving. ⁵For of this you can be sure: No immoral, impure or greedy person—such a person is an idolater—has any inheritance in the kingdom of Christ and of God. ⁶Let no one deceive you with empty words, for because of such things God's wrath comes on those who are disobedient. ⁷Therefore do not be partners with them. ⁸For you were once darkness, but now you are light in the Lord. Live as children of light ⁹(for the fruit of the light consists in all goodness, righteousness, and truth) ¹⁰and find out what pleases the Lord. ¹¹Have nothing to do with the fruitless deeds of darkness, but rather expose them. ¹²It is shameful even to mention what the disobedient do in secret. ¹³But everything exposed by the light becomes visible—and everything that is illuminated becomes a light. ¹⁴This is why it is said:

> "Wake up, sleeper,
> rise from the dead,
> and Christ will shine on you."

¹⁵Be very careful, then, how you live—not as unwise but as wise, ¹⁶making the most of every opportunity, because the days are evil. ¹⁷Therefore do not be foolish, but understand

what the Lord's will is. [18]Do not get drunk on wine, which leads to debauchery. Instead, be filled with the Spirit, [19]speaking to one another with psalms, hymns and songs from the Spirit. Sing and make music from your heart to the Lord, [20]always giving thanks to God the Father for everything, in the name of our Lord Jesus Christ.

Paul makes several commands in this section that plunge to the heart of the Christian life. The guidelines are not simply to do this or avoid that, but rather Paul instructs believers to become in real time what they are already in Christ. And unlike some instructions, such as "shut the door," that a person can accomplish in one step, Paul's instructions to "be" or "follow" (same Greek term *ginomai*, 4:32; 5:1, 7, 17) imply a lifelong process. Further emphasizing the daily transformational goals of imitating God is Paul's repeated call to walk after Christ. Paul insists that a Christian walk in love and truth, not foolishness and sin. The secret to this new attitude is the new person each believer has become. Paul outlined this new life in ch. 4, and now he insists on holy living because believers are God's dearly loved children.

Become Imitators of God (5:1–6)

The audacity of Paul's statement that believers are to imitate God (TNIV: "follow God's example") leads many to write off this verse as an impossible goal. But Paul has a specific focus in mind that he thinks is completely within the believer's capability. In 4:32, believers are enjoined to forgive each other as God forgave them in Christ. Paul focuses on this attitude of forgiveness in his encouragement that believers become imitators of God. The verb implies continuing behavior repeated so as to become habit. This sentiment of forgiveness matches the Lord's Prayer, wherein Jesus taught his disciples to pray, "Forgive us our debts as we also have forgiven our debtors" (Matt 6:12). In 1 Cor 4:16, Paul uses the same verb and noun (become imitators), but there he asks the Corinthians to imitate him. The context is the Corinthians' failure to appreciate Paul's apostolic authority, and also their disregard of his role as their father in the Lord. In both cases, the audience is understood as dear and beloved children. One reason, then, that Paul asks believers in Ephesians to imitate *God* is the connection between God the Father and his children, the church.[1] A second possible reason is that Paul will go on to emphasize walking as *Christ* walked. Finally Paul might be reflecting the charge in Lev 19:2, "Be holy because I, the Lord your God, am holy." Jesus speaks similarly in Matt 5:48, "Be perfect, therefore, as your heavenly father is perfect."[2]

Paul's second command follows closely on the first, and also imagines a daily commitment to act in line with God's truth and love. Believers are to walk in love; this image is found throughout the Old Testament as the manner in which a faithful follower of God lives obediently each day. Everyone can visualize walking; it implies a goal and a gait. The goal is the kingdom of God (5:5). The gait is a pace whose rhythm is love, so one travels as fast or slow as is needed to display charity similar to the self-giving love of Christ. Paul uses this verb repeatedly in ch. 4 as a word picture of the Christian life. Both in 4:1 and now in 5:2, Paul stresses that the believer is to walk in love. As explained in 4:2 and 5:2, this love involves the decision to act humbly, self-sacrificially, and patiently. Christ's love is expressed as a sacrifice on our behalf to God.

Believers are described in this section as dearly loved children (5:1) and as the Lord's people ("holy ones" 5:3), those who will inherit the kingdom of Christ and of God (5:5). Because of their standing before God and their new nature in Christ, the injunctions to love and the warnings against idolatry are possible to live out. The expectation is that just as children imitate their parents because they want to grow up to be just like them, so too children of God will desire to emulate the character of their Father and their Brother. In other words, the moral obligations outlined by Paul are given to those who have been made new so as to fulfill those imperatives.

Walking in love is antithetical to acting with base motives, greed, sexual impropriety, or moral bankruptcy. Walking in love cannot countenance impure language, loud-mouth braggarts, and jokes that shame others. Said positively, believers are distinguished by their moral honor and sexual propriety, by their generosity in speech and action, and by their contentment. In sum, they act in character with the God they worship. This is why Paul can say that greed, fornication, rude jokes, and moral impurity are examples of idolatry—these deeds reflect the character of

1. Paul also speaks of imitating Christ in 1 Cor 11:1 and 1 Thess 1:6.

2. The Greek term translated "perfect" has the sense of being mature or accomplishing the task for which one was made.

false gods. These are acts of disobedience, done, not by children of God, but by "those who are disobedient" (5:6).

The call to walk in love comes with a warning not to be deceived (5:6). What is this deception and who is promoting it? Paul does not reveal who might be arguing that sexual and moral impurity, avarice, and covetousness are of no concern to God. But the deception seems to be centered on a wrong belief about the kingdom of God. Several times in his letters, Paul warns his readers that the immoral person will not inherit God's kingdom. For example, in 1 Cor 6:1–11, the Corinthians are chastised for cheating each other, and for failing to resolve such issues within the church. Paul continues with an extensive list of defining behaviors that expose those who will not inherit God's kingdom. He adds that among the Corinthians, some of them were indeed the drunkards and thieves who had no claim to the kingdom. But, Paul assures them, they now stand washed, sanctified, and justified in the name of Christ and by the Holy Spirit (1 Cor 6:11, see also Gal 5:21). Perhaps it is true in every generation that believers presume on God's love and assume that their behavior has no significance. Paul clearly thought otherwise. Believers—beloved children— simply do not live out their redeemed life in a debauched manner.

Become Wise, Be Filled with the Holy Spirit (5:7–16)

In this section Paul issues eight commands as he distinguishes darkness and light, truth and foolishness, and drunkenness and Spirit-filled living. The call to walk is given again, this time to walk in light. In total, Paul offers four calls to walk[3] as a believer in chs. 4 and 5: walk worthily (4:1), walk in holiness, not as the Gentiles (4:17), walk in love (5:2), and walk in light (5:8). Moreover, Paul will again use the verb "be/become" (5:7, 17) as he further encourages the believers to live out their new reality in Christ. Paul uses a familiar metaphor of fruit to describe deeds both good and bad. He emphasizes light and darkness as stark contrasts of behavior that serve to define character. Three times he cautions the Ephesians not to act one way, but to live in light, understanding, and truth (5:11, 17, 18). Overall, Paul is concerned that the church (being light) presents a sharp contrast to the idolatrous darkness of the wider society.

---

3. TNIV translates the verb in 4:1, 17, and 5:8 as "live."

Paul begins 5:7 with "therefore," which signals he has concluded his previous thought and is now drawing conclusions. He commands that they *not* become actively engaged with those who are disobedient (5:6), for that way is darkness. Paul does not say that the Gentiles are *in* darkness, but that such an existence *is* darkness. The Ephesians should know, Paul reminds them, because this is the life they once led. Perhaps Paul is calling to mind the ninth plague meted out to the Egyptians (Exod 10:21–24). This judgment was a darkness that could be felt, so dark that people could not see each other and had to remain in their homes for three days. This tangible darkness, so thick it had substance, is the thundercloud that encompassed the idolater. Such darkness, however, is not the last word. The Ephesians are now light. Again, they are not *in* light, but are light. Their very substance shines forth the truth of the gospel. This light is truth, holiness, integrity, and love. This light is the life of Jesus Christ, who declares "I am the light of the world" (John 8:12, see also 9:5, 12:35, 46). Paul makes a similar call to the Corinthians in 2 Cor 6:14, 16 when he asks, "what fellowship can light have with darkness?" and further explains his point so that there is no confusion: "what agreement is there between the temple of God and idols?" A similar point is made here: the Ephesians are the light, the witness of the gospel's reconciling power to a world darkened by sin.

A life of light produces rich fruit, all manner of goodness, righteousness, and truth. Paul uses the metaphor of fruit to describe deeds as well in Rom 6:21–22. To the Romans Paul contrasts the fruit (TNIV: "benefit") that is reaped from sin with that produce harvested from acts of righteousness. Fruit is the product of the natural growing cycle. An apple tree will produce apples, not peaches. A fig tree will produce figs, not pineapples. And a believer who is light will produce that which characterizes Christ's life of love and kindness, charity and integrity. But works of darkness, Paul warns, are unfruitful (Eph 5:11).

Paul commands them *not* to participate in such dark works, but rather he urges them to expose such behavior (5:11, 13). This section has been understood in two general ways. One interpretation sees Paul mandating believers to expose by direct, verbal confrontation other believers' sinful behaviors, and thus bring them to repentance.[4] A second view

4. A possible parallel example is 2 Cor 2:5–8. Paul indicates that believers exposed the wrong deed of one of their own, who subsequently repented. Paul encourages the Corinthians to receive back into fellowship the penitent individual.

argues that Paul explains how the believers' godly demeanor and attitude, their "light," exposes the darkness, and transforms it.[5] Verse 5:13 explains 5:11 by describing what happens when light shines on darkness, that is, those deeds done in secret. Light reveals darkness as evil; in so doing, people can see evil for what it really is, and be drawn to light. Isn't this what happened to the Ephesians, as described by Paul in 5:8? Jesus uses similar language in John 3:19–21, while in 1 Cor 14:24–25 Paul applies comparable language when urging the Corinthians to prophesy rather than speak in tongues in their gatherings. The unbeliever will pass by, Paul says, and be convicted by hearing their prophecy. The rebuke here is an implicit one, as the truth of the gospel spoken in the church meeting makes manifest the hidden darkness of the unbeliever's heart. Finally, Paul's hymn in 5:14 brings to mind the call to salvation, reminding the Ephesians of their own conversion. The hymn draws from Isa 26:19[6] and 60:1–2.[7] In Isa 60:1–2, 18–22, God's redemptive acts restore Israel, for God is the Redeemer. Moreover, "nations will come to your light, and kings to the brightness of your dawn" (60:3) holds a promise of Gentiles being drawn into God's people. In Christ, the redemption of Gentiles has been accomplished.

Another command continues the image of light, as Paul orders that the Ephesians *see*[8] very carefully how they walk (5:15), for they must be wise. He follows with a pair of commands that they *not* become foolish, but rather understand the purposes of God. They must realize that the present age is one governed by evil, by attitudes and practices that are antithetical to God's goodness, joy, and redemption. A third pair of commands enjoins the believer *not* to be drunk with wine, but to be filled with the Spirit. Paul contrasts the person wholly controlled by distorted mental and emotional capacities with the one who has completely surrendered to the leading of God's Spirit. In the second case, the person has attained a

---

5. O'Brien 1999: 372.

6. Isa 26:19 reads, "But your dead will live, Lord; their bodies will rise—let those who dwell in the dust wake up and shout for joy—your dew is like the dew of the morning; you will make it fall on the spirits of the dead." The context is restoration, judgment against those who work evil, and blessing to those who walk righteously.

7. Isa 60:1–2 reads, "Arise, shine, for your light has come, and the glory of the Lord rises upon you. See, darkness covers the earth and thick darkness is over the peoples, but the Lord rises upon you and his glory appears over you."

8. This verb is not directly translated in the TNIV.

real and truthful view of the world along with the power to act justly in it (see also Rom 13:11–14; 1 Thess 5:4–11).

Accompanying the command to be filled with the Spirit are several participles that describe what such filling might involve. All these behaviors suppose a community context. A Spirit-filled life is characterized by such deep joy that songs, psalms, and melodies will spring forth. Thankfulness is the constant harmony that supports the daily praises. Paul declares boldly that a Spirit-filled person gives thanks always, and for all things. Since he has clearly acknowledged that the days are evil (5:16) Paul is certainly aware that bad things happen. Are we to be thankful for the bad things? No, but a thankful heart is a faithful one. We are to be thankful in the name of our Lord Jesus Christ, the one who has redeemed us, the one with whom we are raised and seated (2:5–6). We know with absolute assurance that all things are under Christ's feet, and he is head over all (1:22). Though the days are evil and darkness threatens, we walk as ones who see wisely, who know the end of the story, and thus can be thankful.

HOUSEHOLD CODES (5:21–32)

21Submit to one another out of reverence for Christ. 22Wives, submit yourselves to your own husbands as you do to the Lord. 23For the husband is the head of the wife as Christ is the head of the church, his body, of which he is the Savior. 24Now as the church submits to Christ, so also wives should submit to their husbands in everything. 25Husbands, love your wives, just as Christ loved the church and gave himself up for her 26to make her holy, cleansing her by the washing with water through the word, 27and to present her to himself as a radiant church, without stain or wrinkle or any other blemish, but holy and blameless. 28In this same way, husbands ought to love their wives as their own bodies. He who loves his wife loves himself. 29After all, people have never hated their own bodies, but they feed and care for them, just as Christ does the church—30for we are members of his body. 31"For this reason a man will leave his father and mother and be united to his wife, and the two will become one flesh." 32This is a

profound mystery—but I am talking about Christ and the church. [33]However, each one of you also must love his wife as he loves himself, and the wife must respect her husband.

Prolegomena to the Household Codes

I approach the following material as one might when venturing into a minefield. Caution is the order of the day, and adequate preparation. Certain questions should at least be on the table, even if the answers fail to satisfy completely. In Eph 5:21—6:9, Paul addresses marriage, parenting, and slavery. Today far more attention is paid to the first topic, while 150 years ago concentration focused on the third pair, slaves and owners. Having a healthy appreciation for the ancient world's setting is critical to understanding Paul's injunctions; however, it is usually not enough for today's reader, who recognizes "that was then, this is now," at least with respect to slavery. Suggestions follow about what impact Paul's injunctions should have for our lives today and issues of racism and patriarchy float into the conversation. As interpreters of the text, we need to keep an eye both on the historical past and on our own context.

We also need to broaden our approach in several directions. A useful exercise is pondering why Paul included this section at all. He does not bring up marriage, family, or slavery in this way in his other letters, except briefly in Colossians (3:18—4:1). He is not responding to a specific question as he does in 1 Cor 7:1–2, where he discusses sexual behavior in marriage (and mentions slavery briefly, 1 Cor 7:21–23). One way to explore Paul's reasons for including this section is to imagine the letter without it. Picture Paul speaking about being filled with the Spirit (5:21), and going straight to putting on the armor of God (6:10). Would anything be missed? From our vantage point today, given how these verses have been interpreted to sanction abuses against slaves and the promotion of slavery, we might wish they had not been penned. However, for the Ephesians, this section brought their faith down to a livable level. Recall the grand, liturgical sounding language in chs. 1 and 2 that lauded God the Father, the Lord Jesus, and the Holy Spirit. The surety of a believer's salvation, the certainty of being seated with Christ, and the promise that all will end well, these are all truths to be treasured. Paul's burden in chs. 4 and 5 is to help believers live out their salvation. He begins in the church, explaining the importance of gifts for building up the community. Next he contrasts the Gentile way of life, the life of debauchery, idolatry, greed, and selfishness witnessed in the marketplace and the temples, with the godly life in the Spirit. But we all know that the rubber meets the road in the family, and so to be thorough, Paul must explain what life in the Spirit looks like within the household. But by seeing the household codes as private ethics, we gain only half the historical picture. The household in the ancient world was the center of city life, and intimately connected, politically and economically, on an actual and theoretical level with the city.

Because the household was a central piece of political discussions, a second issue emerges, namely, whether Paul hopes believers will blend in and not give offense in their roles as spouses, family members, and slaves/owners or whether he is promoting another vision of the household. An analogous question animates studies of 1 Peter. This epistle has a similarly lengthy discussion about the household that encourages all to submit to the emperor, who was known as the Father of the Empire, and for slaves to submit to their masters, and wives to their husbands (1 Pet 2:13—3:7). Some suggest that Peter hoped to secure acceptance of the gospel through conforming to or linking with the wider cultural structures. Others argue that Peter challenged his readers to stand against the temptation to assimilate. When we ask the same questions of Ephesians, I suggest that we find Paul concerned that the Ephesians *not* assimilate or mimic the surrounding culture, but rather implicitly critique it by living out the demands of the gospel. He configures the argument to make obvious that a Spirit-filled life is not bound to the social constructions established in this present age.

Exploration into why Paul addresses the household also opens up the opportunity to examine the theology in this section. Paul's emphasis in this letter has been Christ and the church, or said another way, on soteriology, Christology, and ecclesiology. His specific burden has been explaining the penultimate chapter in God's redemptive story wherein through Christ God has made a people for himself from both Jews and Gentiles. The unity of the two stands as a witness to God's greatness and salvific power. A similar emphasis on unity (of husband and wife) permeates the household codes. Although today we might read Paul's statement about Christ being the head of the church and its Savior as a convenient illustration of marriage, it is more likely that a particular aspect of marriage (the unique union of two becoming one) served to elicit yet another image of Christ's work and person for the earliest believers.

The Ancient Society

Two key concepts of ancient society must be understood when interpreting the household codes. The first is the honor/shame culture. To use a computer analogy, this would be the hardware; honor/shame categories control the possibilities within the system. The various programs running on the computer can be likened to the hierarchical society whose organization was based on status, reciprocity, and benefaction. Additionally, the political realm was rooted organically in the household structure. These forces together meant that the highest goal for any person was to achieve honor, and the path to honor lay in submitting to authority or those of higher status. Shame was the lot of those who sought an individual road, or who failed to praise their benefactor, or who stepped outside the socially drawn lines of conduct for their station in life. Each of these aspects of ancient culture must be appreciated to better interpret Paul's injunctions to the Ephesians.

Honor/Shame Culture

Looking first at the honor/shame culture,[9] this approach to human interaction focuses on group values, which are determined and enforced by the community. Honorable behaviors are those that further the community's goals; disgraceful deeds are those that put the community at risk. In Paul's world, people did not make sense of themselves as individuals but as members of a larger group. One's identity was embedded in the family or the city. For example, a female's identity and honor was rooted in a male's honor, and a child's honor was embedded in their father or mother's honor. In the West we tend to internalize our norms and focus on what is right and wrong; we do not seek the explicit approval of the larger group. We encourage individualism and risk-taking for personal gain. We value difference and independence. Yet in the military and in sporting competitions we find something of the honor/shame culture today. Athletes representing their countries in the modern Olympic games are rewarded by their fellow countrymen not with monetary gain, but with social honor and respect. We feel ashamed of those who act cowardly or those who during the sporting event do not give their all for the team's victory.

9. For a useful explanation of the honor/shame culture as it impacts the New Testament, see DeSilva 2000.

A distinctive of an honor/shame culture is its assumption that honor is a limited good, and thus should be contested. The ancient honor/shame culture was a zero-sum game inasmuch as one gained honor while another was shamed. This aspect of the culture is known as the challenge-riposte, and it involved a challenge being leveled to which the other needed to respond. Failure to meet the test adequately brought shame, but a superior response disgraced the challenger, who might extend another challenge to regain lost honor. Additionally, any dishonorable misdeeds by wives, children, or slaves brought shame to the husband, parents, or owners. No one stood on their own merits entirely, but could be brought low by their relations. For example, a child's failure to be courageous or intelligent plagued the parents whose family honor depended upon their child fulfilling expectations.

The poignant story of the rape of Lucretia is saturated with the ideals of honor/shame. In this tale about the political overthrow of ancient Rome's king and the establishment of Roman republican government, we find several young men from leading families and princes boasting about the chasteness of their wives. They decide to prove to each other the respectability of their own wives by leaving the besieged city to check on them. It is late in the evening, and all the wives but one are preparing for a banquet (nothing specifically immoral is suggested). Only one wife, Lucretia, is still busy working, spinning wool in her home. Her industry brought much honor to her husband, Collantinus, but it shamed the other men. Angry at being shamed, one of these princes, Sextus Tarquinius, returned to the house a few nights later and raped her. The next morning, she sent word to her father and husband, who returned with a few friends. They believed her recounting of the story, but she feared that other women in the future might use her name to justify an extramarital affair. To end all possible doubt as to her innocence, she committed suicide. Her death was avenged with the overthrow of the monarchy and the establishment of the Roman Republic. Two pulses of this story continued to pound in Paul's day: the fear of monarchical rule and the importance of women working in their homes. Thus the first Emperor, Augustus, was at pains to present himself not as a supreme ruler but as a traditionalist who acceded to the wishes of the Senate. He spoke of his wife, Livia, as one who worked with wool and made his clothes. Neither of these presentations reflected the actual situation, but the values Augustus expressed were driven deep into the culture of his day.[10]

10. Cohick 2009: 71–78.

Social Stratification

The honor/shame culture relied on defined roles so that individuals knew to whom they owed honor. Social categorization was critical, with status and rank emphasized.[11] This interest in social taxonomy reflected the wider search for understanding the natural world. The modern saying "everything has a place, and there is a place for everything" would have resonated well in the Greco-Roman world. The ancient Greeks, and later the Hellenists and the Romans, were fascinated with their physical environment, and sought to categorize and catalogue the physical world into groups and sub-groups. Aristotle believed that nature had created an order, and humans were to live out that ordering for the sake of the home and the city (the political unit in Aristotle's day was the city-state). He concluded that male was the pinnacle of the created order, with female inferior in all ways (both physical and intellectual), and slaves likewise not fit to make decisions but to follow orders. The Hellenistic world followed Aristotle's lead.[12] They sought to understand the Mind of the universe represented in the logical order that sustained life. Chaos was greatly feared, and every attempt to keep order was pursued. Hierarchy existed at all levels, as philosophers and scientists created taxonomies of species, classifications of heavenly bodies, and analyses of social and natural events.

Within this carefully constructed system, however, we find some movement. For example, a good soldier might rise in the ranks, as did the equestrian Vespasian whose military feats gained him senatorial ranking, and then the office of emperor (he ruled from 69–79 CE). Sadly, the fates might tip against one, as they did the auxiliary soldier Spartacus from Thrace (Greece). He apparently deserted, was captured by Rome, and subjected to slavery by the very group he had earlier fought to protect. We know him best today as the gladiator who led a large uprising against Rome. His hope of escaping Italy and returning home failed, and he and his fellow slaves were slaughtered. But the story of their revolt made slave masters' blood run cold, and the fear of being killed by one's own slaves continued to haunt masters down to Paul's day.

11. For a detailed discussion exploring how social status impacted women, see Cohick 2009: 285–320.

12. Cohick 2009: 66–69.

Benefaction and Reciprocity

In sum, society was highly stratified, and one's place on the social hierarchy had political and economic repercussions. This basic understanding of society characterized Paul's day, and the honor/shame code permeated both the Jewish and the Gentile communities. The ordering of society into status levels and rank were supported by an ontological assessment of the nature of each person and group, based largely on Aristotle's conclusions, although the Jews' assessment about what was honorable was shaped as well by the Old Testament. This stratified culture supported a second important social construct, that of benefaction. Essentially, benefaction is the giving of gifts. It requires reciprocity, such that one who gives the gift has placed the receiver in their debt. The patron or gift giver must be honored for his beneficence by the client or recipient. If possible, the client should repay the patron financially, but often that was impossible as the client was poorer than the patron. This meant that the client was beholden to the patron, and was expected to publicly praise and offer tribute to their patron. This system of reciprocity is especially important when we consider the household codes, because most thinkers in Paul's day assumed that a wife, child, or slave could not benefit their husband, father, or master, for that would alter the asymmetrical relationship. Instead, any aid done by wife or child was understood as their duty, while any such deed done by the slave was his or her service to the owner.

We see the system of reciprocity sketched out in Seneca,[13] a first-century CE Stoic philosopher. He discusses the order of society as it relates to receiving benefits, noting that most believe that only a stranger can give a benefit, because only a stranger is able to discontinue benefits without blame. This is contrasted with wives and children, whose duties to their husbands or fathers are inherent in the relationship, and slaves, whose relationship with their masters is such that no deed could ever be considered a gift that would put the master in their debt. Seneca argues against this assumption by noting that some slaves give their lives to protect their masters; clearly this is above the duty of a slave, and thus is a gift. Moreover, Seneca argues that while the slave's body is caged, the mind is free to follow virtue.

Yet even with this sound critique, neither Seneca nor other philosophers attacked the institution itself. The conditions of slavery were debated by some philosophers because they knew that at least some slaves were not born into

13. Seneca *Ben.* 3:18–29.

slavery, but had been free men with social standing (before pirates or a military defeat changed their fate).[14] Thus even at this time, the theoretical underpinnings of slavery were a bit shaky. That said, for the most part, philosophers only chided slave owners to refrain from brutalizing their slaves because, they argued, these slaves were human beings, after all. This is the burden of Seneca's lengthy discussion about the mistreatment of slaves.[15] After he decries the debauchery and excess of owners, which speaks of their own slavery to their passions, he states that vicious beatings do nothing to make a slave better at his task. Seneca declares that the owner should not expect his slave to fear him, but respect him. Yet when his imaginary interlocutor exclaims that Seneca has essentially awarded the slave manumission, Seneca disagrees. He steps away from the possibility that the institution of slavery is flawed, content to state only that the hierarchy is acceptable, and should not be abused. The reasons preventing the next step from being taken include the economic role of slaves, especially in Rome, and a conviction that a slave was born or destined by fate to be a slave. However, because people could move in and out of slavery for a number of reasons, it was difficult to state categorically that a male slave's soul was discernibly different from a freeborn male's. And so the tension remained, as did the institution of slavery.

A similar tension was faced about 150 years ago in the United States, with abolitionists pitted against those who supported the institution of slavery. The reasons for the Civil War are many and varied, but our purpose here is to call attention to the theological debates that engaged both Northern and Southern Christians. The country faced a theological crisis, not because people did not believe in God or the Bible, but because their hermeneutical tools left them unprepared to deal with this social issue. Their difficulties in part lay in their assumption that the Bible was a simple book that took only common sense to interpret. This led to ignoring the Bible's own historical context and social assumptions, and instead reading it as though it was a set of propositions to be applied trans-culturally. Today we require an agile hermeneutic that contends with context without being completely determined by it.

---

14. For example, see Dio Chrysostom 2 *Serv. lib.* 15.26–32.
15. Seneca *Ep.* XLVII.

Household Codes (5:21—6:9)

Believers walk in the Spirit; they speak psalms, sing and make melody in their hearts, give thanks always, and submit. The Spirit-filled life imagined by Paul is one of deep joy that bubbles to the surface where it runs over blessing others. Such a life is lived in community, celebrating God the Father in the name of the Lord Jesus Christ. I want to pause a moment and let this vision sink in. We will move to one of the most contentious passages of Scripture next, the household codes. So we need to stop for a moment and realize that the Spirit-filled life, the life of joy and thanksgiving, moves out from the church into the social ordering of relationships. This larger world included for Paul basic human structures such as parent and child, as well as social institutions such as slavery. And it included marriage, which, like parent and child, is a basic human relationship that each society shapes to fit its political, economic, and cultural values. It is onto the first-century social grid that Paul places the ethics of Christ with its amazing transformative powers to redeem human attitudes and perspectives.

Into the Greco-Roman cultural construct, Paul speaks of Christ's model of love and of the Christian ethic. Some imagine this love as a coat placed over the body politic, the Roman society and social institutions. The coat molds itself to the person and serves not to critique the body, but to adjust to it and protect it from harm. A conclusion is then drawn from the analogy that Christian ethics rehabilitate the social structures of marriage and parenting and slavery, getting rid of the abuses that come from sin. Indeed, this approach was active in the slavery debate a century or so ago in the United States. The institution was salvageable, so long as it wore the coat of Christian ethics. However, this is not Paul's message. The coat of Christian ethics is one that changes the underlying body. Rather than the coat conforming to the body and improving its capabilities to keep warm, the coat of Christ's love, the Spirit-filled coat, actually changes the body to conform to it. We have examples of these sorts of coats or body wrappings. I remember in high school watching wrestlers desperate to make weight run in rubber sweat suits, and seeing ads for women's girdles designed to pull in the belly. These "coats" changed the body, though only temporarily. The change Paul imagines is permanent, as we saw in 4:24, as Christians put on their new self. Paul is not suggesting that Christ is accommodating himself to us, but rather that in wearing Christ, we begin to change. If we carry this analogy forward to social ethics, we have Paul suggesting a covering of Christ's ethics over all social relationships—not to preserve them, but to change and renew them.

Wives and Husbands Addressed (5:21–33)[16]

Wives Submit to Husbands (5:22–24)

Verses 5:21–24 focuses on two key terms, "submit" and "head," upon which the interpretation of these verses hinge. Turning to the first term, "submit," by now the reader is familiar with the stratified Greco-Roman culture embraced to a greater or lesser extent by Jews and Gentiles alike. For example, submitting to authorities was as natural as breathing, and just as critical for the existence of ordered society. Paul's language of submission, therefore, was easily understood in its larger context, because everyone submitted to someone else, even the Emperor, who submitted to the gods. Within almost every relationship there was a superordinate and a subordinate, and examples include patron/client and master/slave. The ordering implied a valuation, such that the patron, master, and male was seen as superior. However, the second element of the pair was judged to be necessary, for without it there was no harmony, no social order. I should note that a patron or master could be female, and her client or slave a male, which means that subordination in the ancient world was not limited to male/female.

A close reading of Paul's injunctions suggests that he shapes the common understanding so that believers comprehend their actions as unto Christ. Although each person is new in Christ, the present relationships that govern social order in the family, namely marriage, parenting, and slavery, must still be negotiated. In the present age of the Roman Empire (which is passing away), hierarchy and stratification keep order, and order is a good thing. Totalitarian government, such as the Roman Empire, was deemed much better than no government at all, and, ironically to our way of thinking, democracy was seen as little better than mob rule (Rom 13:1–7, 1 Pet 2:13–17). Indeed, in one peculiar use of the terms "order" and "submit," Paul tells the men and women prophets in Corinth

---

16. For a general discussion of marriage in the Greco Roman world, see Cohick 2009: 65–131.

that the spirit of prophecy submits to the speaker, for God is a God of order (1 Cor 14:32–33).

One of the first things the reader notes when looking at the text in Greek is that the verb is lacking in 5:22. The verb must be taken from 5:21, and so many see 5:21 as a bridge between the comments about being filled with the Spirit and living in the household. We saw that 5:18 contained the commands to not be drunk with wine but filled with the Spirit. Several participles follow, including the phrase in 5:21 about submitting to each other out of fear of Christ. The English translations often change the participle into the indicative (submit) but that can separate 5:21 from the main verb clause in 5:18. Paul connects through the use of participles his insistence on life in the Spirit with his discussion about submission.

The social conventions of his day limit Paul's options as he instructed the church, much as a sculptor is limited by the shape and color of her stone and the painter is limited by the size of his canvas. Paul's words would carry certain shared meanings that fit the context. So what does Paul mean that believers submit to each other (5:21)? This sounded like a contradiction because submission implied a loss of status for the one who submits. But for Paul, status is tied to being in Christ, and since all are of equal status in Christ, then no one loses face when submitting to another. Indeed, Paul's revolutionary insight is that if the believer's life is hid in Christ, if the believer died in Christ and is raised to new life, then submitting to another believer was merely submitting to Christ himself. To the Corinthians Paul explains that the body of Christ, while it has many members, does not rank those members based on social status or value them based on their ancestry (1 Cor 12:7–26). To the ancient mind, this was a recipe for chaos, but Paul assures the Corinthians that the Spirit will give leadership gifts and will expect each to look to the benefit of the whole (1 Cor 12:27—13:8; 14:29–33).

With its call for believers to submit to each other, the verb in 5:21 governs 5:22 and its instructions for wives to submit to their own husbands as to the Lord. Note that Paul qualifies "submit" in both verses: in 5:21 with the phrase "out of reverence for Christ" and in 5:22 as "to the Lord." Paul pictures each believer as submitting to Christ, and that is shown by submitting to the other members of Christ's body. This participle can be interpreted as either middle or passive (being submissive or submitting yourselves), which affects the interpretation. The passive voice would imply that the person instructed has little say in the matter, while the middle implies some agency. This latter sense is preferred, as it matches the other active participles' voice and it fits Paul's point that believers should not act as though drunk (passively under the influence of another source) but actively make choices following the Spirit's leading.

A second key term is "head," a metaphor used here to describe the husband and Christ.[17] The metaphor aligns the wife with "body," although this is not stated directly. The metaphorical use of both "head" and "body" have been used earlier in Ephesians, always with "head" referring to Christ and "body" to the church (1:22–23, 4:15–16). Because we have become so accustomed to hearing this language, it loses its vibrant force, but when Paul wrote, he chose these words to create new meaning by linking two concepts that had not been connected before in people's imaginations. Today we often read "head" and in our minds substitute "leader" because that is how the metaphor is used in English; indeed one could argue that today "head" has ceased to be a metaphor. But in Paul's day, this metaphor was not a fixed symbol with a literal meaning. Paul's thrust took its power from connecting two different ideas (such as husband and wife) via the metaphors of "head" and "body" to create a new argument. Paul uses the literal subjects of Christ, wife, and husband as the frame, together with the non-literal meanings of "head" and "body," to create his dynamic metaphor expounding upon unity. We should resist the temptation to assume that a metaphor can be easily replaced by an equivalent literal expression, for an intrinsic part of the metaphor is its creative punch, its ability to excite the imagination and extend the boundaries of possibilities.

Paul's focus in using this metaphor can be understood in two ways. Either Paul is interested in ethical injunctions or in describing the analogical relationship between marriage and Christ and the church. The two are not mutually exclusive, but the second makes better sense of the curious phrase that Christ is the Savior of the body (5:23). This phrase clearly distinguishes Christ's headship from the husband's headship, thus narrowing the application of the latter.

Why use body imagery here? When we glance back at the use of "head" in 1:22–23, we find that "head" and "feet" create a vivid picture of Christ's surpassing glory and dominion over all forces. The term "head" is used here as the complement to "feet"; the image of the vanquished at the conqueror's feet is a common one, readily apprehended. A second

---

17. Cohick 2007: 93–97.

use of Christ as head is in 4:15–16, where Paul's burden is describing the growth and maturity of the church, Christ's body. Note the organic connection between the head and the body, as well as the emphasis on wisdom, unity, and love. In 5:22–24, Christ as head is explained in part as Christ the Savior, a quality that is not characteristic of husbands. Three reasons might have prompted Paul to use the "head" and "body" metaphors. First, he is still thinking of life in the Spirit (5:18), and the image of the church as Christ's body comes naturally to mind. Second, he is preparing the way for his argument about husbands and wives being one body in 5:28–31. Finally, using "head" and "body" allows Paul to create a dynamic metaphor that further explains the all-embracing union of Christ and his church.

What is Paul implying with these metaphors?[18] Some argue that the language of "head" implies that the husband is the *source* of goodness and help for his wife. The term "Savior" used to describe Christ is understood to reflect the husband's role as protector for the wife, who did not have at that time the legal and social protections of a man. Others suggest that "head" means leader, indicating that Paul's focus is on the natural hierarchy between male and female which is expressed in the marriage relationship. The hierarchical scheme assumed with the use of the participle "submit" suggests that Paul's interest is focused sharply on the idea of respect and honor due to the one who is superordinate. Paul ends the discourse on wives and husbands with a call for the wife to respect (fear) her husband (5:33), which is the expected attitude or posture of one who submits. Paul's language should not conjure up a military image of a commander over his troops, giving orders for the enlisted to follow. His point is that wives must honor their husbands, and to honor someone is to submit to them.

One final point should be noted. Very few ancient writers use the term "submit" when describing the role of the wife, although the concept of submission was widespread. Thus the superficial sense of Paul's injunction, that wives owe their husbands submission, would have seemed self-evident to his readers. However, Paul's specific vocabulary (using the participle from 5:21, restricting "head" as only limitedly similar to Christ's position as head, and using the qualifier "as to the Lord") all serve to nuance his position in ways he develops further in his argument.

18. For a similar discussion from 1 Cor 11:3, see ibid., 94.

Husbands Love Your Wives (5:25–33)

Paul's lengthy charge that husbands love their wives includes several important features. First, while the term "body" (*soma*) is carried over from the verses above, the term "head" is not. Moreover, he shifts from using "body" metaphorically to speaking literally of the physical body in the course of his argument. Related to this is Paul's use of the term "flesh" (*sarx*), which further reinforces the literal sense of "body." Second, Paul speaks of similarity and unity as opposed to distinction and difference as he did in his charge to wives. Third, Paul focuses extensively on Christ's love and self-giving for the church. Fourth, the work of Christ for the church has eschatological dimensions, for the church will be presented to Christ as holy and blameless. Fifth, Christ's relationship to the church is a mystery in its unity and oneness.

Unlike the charge to wives, where the participle "submit" is carried over from the previous verse, in 5:25 Paul commands husbands to love their wives. The verb is the cognate of the noun *agapē*, the self-giving love characterizing Christ's love for the church. A husband's love is more than romantic feelings, although these feelings were an expected part of marriage. Paul describes this love as self-giving (5:25) and, ironically, as self-referential (5:28) inasmuch as the husband is to love his wife as he loves himself. Additionally, while the husband is to love his wife as Christ does the church, the result of this love differs. The husband's love is shown in the care given to his wife, while Christ's love is redemptive and sanctifying, and carries eschatological power (5:26).

Paul connects his first call for the husband to love his wife with Christ's love and self-giving for the church. The second charge to love one's wife gives a reason for this behavior. Paul declares that a husband and wife are one body, thus the husband should show the same regard for his wife as he shows for himself. Paul speaks both metaphorically and literally here when using "body." And to expand on both meanings, he introduces the term "flesh." He speaks of the husband's literal flesh which is fed and clothed, and metaphorically of the wife as one flesh with her husband. This metaphor provides the opportunity to bring in the description of marriage in Gen 2:24. The New Testament (following the LXX) adjusts the Old Testament language by saying that "the *two* become one flesh," (see Matt 19:5). This shift modifies the Hebrew "*they* shall become one flesh," which accommodated polygyny. By the Hellenistic period monogamy was common among Jews and promoted by the Greeks and Romans, who outlawed bigamy. Evidence indicates that a few Jews practiced polygyny, but that arrangement was not recognized by Roman courts.

For Paul, the unity of the couple, their oneness of flesh, is squarely rooted in the Genesis account. The Greeks and Romans would have admitted as well that the whole takes precedent over the parts. Aristotle noted that unity is prior to division. In an example, he noted that a hand is only a hand if it is connected to a body. If one removes a hand or foot from the body, they cease to be functional hands or feet but are similar to sculptured stone.[19] Thus although in his discussion of marriage, Paul first notes the distinction between head and body, his conclusions in the second half of the argument stress unity, from which distinctions can be made. The quality of difference makes Paul's claim of unity so outstanding. As we have seen in previous chapters, the unity of Christ's body is made manifest in the oneness of Jew and Gentile. Here the view has shifted slightly, with the emphasis on the unity reflected in the oneness of husband and wife. The key note of unity which has sounded throughout the epistle rises in volume with the marriage metaphor. Even more, Paul reshapes the body metaphor of husband/wife so that it covers the entire body of Christ. Thus the theme of unity and the body/flesh metaphors serve three related images: husband and wife as one flesh, individual believers united in one body, and Christ united with the church, his body.

A surprising possibility emerges from Paul's argument. If the husband is one flesh with his wife, as Paul declares, could the same be said of the wife to her husband? If the husband loves his wife, who is his own body, it seems logically possible that the wife could love her husband, who is her own body.[20] A measure of reciprocity is latent in Paul's image here, but it is explicit in 1 Cor 7:4, where Paul notes that the wife does not have authority over her own body, but her husband does, and the husband does not have authority over his own body, but the wife does. In the end, both married partners take their identity as members of Christ's body, to whom they are united through his love. This is the power of the gospel, which unsettles the status quo and lifts up the humble.

19. Aristotle *Pol.* 1253a.
20. Dawes 1998: 205.

Fusing the Horizons: Marriage Then and Now

Given the strains on marriage today, how does the redemptive message of the gospel build up couples? Marriage is unique among relationships in creating one flesh from two, thus it provides the best parallel for understanding Christ's intimacy with the church. While the fall marred God's creation, with the coming of Christ, God's kingdom has been inaugurated. In Christ couples enjoy the hope of new life individually and as one flesh. God's story of redemption includes his promises to make each believer new in Christ, redeemed and no longer a slave to sin. The new self (Eph 4:24) speaks truthfully, and works through anger and resentment each day, allowing nothing to fester (4:26–27). The believer's speech is redemptive, uplifting, focused on benefiting others. The Christian marriage testifies to the power of God, which makes the two one, witnessing to God's reconciling power making the church one with Christ.

Summary of 5:21–33

The analogies used by Paul above, that marriage should resemble the relationship of Christ and the church, are not bothersome to most Christians. Additionally, Christians have been encouraged to love and serve each other, based on Christ's example. The troubling aspect of the marriage discussion is Paul's use of the metaphors "head" and "body" because they support an asymmetrical relationship between husband and wife (based on the patriarchal view of male superiority and superordination). While these two terms reflect the traditional viewpoint of the wider culture, Paul weakens their force by connecting the call for wives' submission to that of the wider church's demand that believers, filled with the Spirit, submit to each other as reflecting their newness in Christ. The traditional view is further weakened with Paul's use of "body" and "flesh," for the emphasis is on the oneness of the married couple, not the dissimilarity between them. Their very distinctiveness as male and female opens the possibility for them to become one flesh. The husband's wife is as his own flesh, for they are one flesh, which implies that the wife's husband is as her own flesh. Through this image, Paul has introduced reciprocity in marriage. This Christian distinctive, grounded in the charges to the first couple (Gen

2:24), connects to the eschatological vision of Christ and the church as inextricably united. The mystery of God's will (1:9), that Gentiles are co-heirs with Jews in Christ, one body (3:3–9), has a further dimension. The marriage of two becoming one develops into a sign of the unity of Christ and the church, effective now and to be fully consummated in the end.

As exemplified in the institution of slavery discussed in the following chapter, the way the ancient world ordered its society need not be implemented today. I suggest that the institution of patriarchy, which infused the social ordering of men and women, is destabilized by this passage. Moreover, Paul's goal is not only to shed light on marriage, but to emphasize the supernatural mystery of which marriage serves as an analogy. Paul probes the depths of the relationship between Christ and the church, the unity shared by the body of believers, joined inseparably together and to the head, Christ. The organic, visual impact of this image should give each believer a rock solid confidence in their own security in Christ, as well as appreciation for the far-reaching importance of embracing the life of community with other believers as the church.

EPHESIANS 6

This chapter includes a continuation of the household codes as well as a final call to the saints to stand fast, ready in the face of an expected assault by the evil that characterizes the present age. The chapter divisions do a disservice to the flow of Paul's thought on the household by separating his comments on marriage in chapter 5 from his remarks to parents/children and slaves/masters in chapter 6. The arrangement does serve to stress, however, the connection between our daily home lives with the wider reality of spiritual activity present in our midst. After concluding our discussion of the household codes, we will explore in more depth the call to take up the armor of God.

HOUSEHOLD CODES CONTINUED (6:1–9)

[1]Children, obey your parents in the Lord, for this is right. [2]"Honor your father and mother"—which is the first commandment with a promise—[3]"so that it may go well with you and that you may enjoy long life on the earth." [4]Fathers, do not exasperate your children; instead, bring them up in the training and instruction of the Lord. [5]Slaves, obey your earthly masters with respect and fear, and with sincerity of heart, just as you would obey Christ. [6]Obey them not only to win their favor when their eye is on you, but as slaves of Christ, doing the will of God from your heart. [7]Serve wholeheartedly, as if you were serving the Lord, not people, [8]because you know that the Lord will reward each one of you for whatever good you do, whether you are slave or free. [9]And masters, treat your slaves in the same way. Do not threaten them, since you know that he who is both their Master and yours is in heaven, and there is no favoritism with him.

Children and Parents Addressed (6:1–4)

The second twosome of the household codes seems unproblematic on first read, and compared with the other two pairs, its interpretation is less contentious. However, the force of the injunction is muted in our Western culture, probably in part because we value youth and innovation while labeling the older members of society as behind the times and even a burden on the society. My years in Kenya showed me another way entirely to understand the obedience of children to parents and the attitudes underpinning the call to honor parents. The African culture is instructive in that it mirrors Paul's environment in many respects. Contemporary Asian cultures as well have a much higher regard for honoring parents, and they come to our text with a better appreciation for Paul's injunctions.

Paul instructs children to obey their parents. The verb's present tense is in the command form, suggesting that this is a posture children should take because God commanded it. Obviously, Paul is not advocating that a child obey a parent who asks them to sin, nor is Paul suggesting that the child have no dreams or aspirations of their own. Rather, the child is enjoined to respect his or her parents as they model the wisdom and grace of God that they experienced in their lives. Paul quotes from the Decalogue (using the Greek translation, Exod 20:12; Deut 5:16). No person, Jew or Gentile, would dispute Paul's claims that children should honor and obey their parents. So why does he add that the commandment includes a promise of blessing for obedient children? Most likely Paul adds the promise because this phrase is in the biblical text. God's command for children to honor parents is sweetened with his promise to honor the obedient ones with long life. As the child grows to adulthood, they remain the progeny of their parents, and as such, they continue to obey and honor them, although the specific deeds of obedience might look different. And each culture negotiates the level of involvement expected by parents. In some settings, parents choose their children's spouses, and have extensive influence over where their children live and what occupations they take up. In the West such involvement is generally not reinforced by the wider culture, but perhaps some modification from our individualism might be helpful. In this endeavor, our sisters and brothers in Africa and the East can be important resources.

While the command to obey includes both parents, the charge to refrain from exasperating children is addressed to the fathers. It is possible that mothers are assumed here. However, since a mother's authority is generally limited by a male family member, it may be that they had fewer opportunities to frustrate a child. Paul enjoins fathers to train their children in the Lord. It is a truism that more men than women had education at this time; however, mothers were also praised for educating or overseeing the education of their sons. Paul is not implying that mothers should not teach their children, rather that fathers should be actively involved. Jewish and Roman authors agreed in praising fathers who took a hand in training or supervising their children's education. Education looked very different depending on one's status and finances. Wealthy families educated both sons and daughters. For example, we know that male philosophers trained their sons and daughters in their craft. Poorer families would train their children in the family business, for most children continued the work of their parents. Also, an owner raising a foundling might send him off to learn a trade such as weaving. I mention the latter example because households might include the parents' children and slave children. Often they were raised together, at least in the early years, for the slave children were the owner's property and were worth taking care of and educating.

Fusing the Horizons: Infanticide and Abortion

Amidst the similarities between a Jewish and Gentile family there is one glaring difference: the practice of infanticide. Jews (and later Christians) spoke with one voice against the practice of exposing newborn children as tantamount to murder. The wider Roman world defended the practice as reasonable and logical. Perhaps an evil omen occurred at birth, warning the father not to raise the child, or perhaps the child's legitimacy was in question. Other writers complained that some fathers were too lazy or greedy to raise more than one or two children, and so destroyed subsequent infants.[1] Weak or deformed infants, both male and female, were left to the elements outside the town, or were drowned.[2] The poor might expose their infants because they lacked the money to educate them, and a life with no education is one without any virtue,

1. Polybius *Hist.* 36.17.5–8.
2. Seneca *Ira* 1.15.

and thus shameful.[3] While our society today does not countenance the exposure of infants, many point to abortion, which has claimed untold numbers of children, as a parallel. Many churches' positions today against the dominant rationales for abortion, which are similar to the defenses given for infanticide, stand in line with its ancient witness to the inviolability of life.

The New Testament itself does not directly speak about abortion, perhaps because this procedure was not practiced among Jews, and apparently was infrequent among Gentiles because of the risks to the mother. Yet if we look at the larger picture of the New Testament story, we hear a chord that sounds against the practice.[4] First, the New Testament indicates that life is from God (John 1:3–5), and life is a gift. Second, humans are called to be stewards of life. Third, Christ died for all human life, including that which lives *in utero*. How did Jesus and the earliest community live out these realities? Jesus cites the Good Samaritan as an example of aiding those who are helpless and needy. Paul calls on believers to imitate Christ, who himself gave his life for needy humanity.[5] The church today has the opportunity to extend aid in several ways. First, it must embrace women who have had abortions as loved by God; judgmental attitudes have no place in the church. Second, it must care for mothers who are unable to care for their children. Third, it should promote adoption. The church today might echo Mother Teresa's plea at the National Prayer Breakfast in 1994, "And for this I appeal in India and I appeal everywhere: 'Let us bring the child back.'"

Slaves and Masters Addressed (6:5–9)

The stains of slavery in America color our perspective on ancient slavery and impact our interpretation of biblical passages on the matter. Retaining slavery after the Revolutionary War was the great failing[6] of the founding fathers, who admitted as much even to themselves but left

3. Plutarch *Am. prol.* 5.

4. I am speaking here in general terms; I recognize that social concerns (for example, rape) and medical issues (for example, imminent death of the mother) surrounding a particular pregnancy might raise the need to consider terminating the pregnancy.

5. Hays 1996: 449–61.

6. The failure to establish longstanding treaties with the Native Americans is a second, closely related failure, which was likewise recognized by Washington, Jefferson, and others.

it to subsequent generations to rid the country of such terror. From our perspective today, it seems common sense that no person should own another, so how did the early Americans justify the practice? A second question follows, namely how did later pro-slavery and abolitionists read their Bibles concerning slavery? These questions will be examined after looking at Paul's injunctions to slaves and owners.

In Paul's day, slavery was not based on race or religion, but on fate, chance, or birth. Defeated armies and peoples were enslaved, those captured by pirates were held as slaves, and many slaves were born to slave mothers. Slaves might be better educated than a free man or woman, have better living accommodations and might hope to gain their freedom, and with it, Roman citizenship. These slaves were household slaves living with wealthy families, and might even own slaves themselves. Other slaves rowed in galley ships, worked in mines or in fields, and died in the gladiatorial games. Yet all slaves shared this in common: they were owned by another. Their low status extended to the marketplace and public venues, where they were expected to honor all free and freed people. For many, the slave was an animal with a voice that could be abused with impunity. Owners had sexual access to both their male and female slaves, and their behavior towards slaves was known to be rough and indecent. Many prostitutes (male and female) were slaves. Husbands were not to treat their wives as they did their slaves, as seen in a first-century CE divorce filing wherein the wife defended the separation because her husband treated her as he did his slave.[7]

In Paul's injunction to slaves, several points should be noted. First, Paul speaks directly to slaves, something not seen outside the New Testament. Greco-Roman authors spoke to masters about treating slaves kindly, but never addressed slaves directly. Second, Paul commands that slaves obey their masters, but he does not stop with that injunction for he would be telling them nothing they did not already know. Paul expounds on what this obedience looks like. He asks that they assume a posture of fear and trembling. A similar request was made to wives, that they fear (respect) their husbands (5:33). In Phil 2:12, Paul asks that all believers work out their salvation with fear and trembling, a posture suitable before God. Thus in Paul's time, fear or respect is that which is owed to the per-

---

7. Glancy 2002: 21.

son above you in the social hierarchy. Paul stresses that fear and respect is the proper attitude owed by humans to their God.

Paul observes that slaves actually have two masters: the earthly master, who may or may not be charitable and kind, and a heavenly Master who is just, good, rewards generously, and who is the Master of their owner as well. They should look to this second master when performing their tasks in obedience to their earthly owner. As is true of any believer doing a task, the focus is on humility of heart before Christ. Paul cautions them not to serve only when the master is watching, thereby giving a false impression of their work ethic. Their service should come from their heart, which is set on Christ's promises that good and faithful labor will be rewarded. He uses similar language when writing to the Galatians about his apostleship. He asks them whether his gospel message indicates that he is trying to please people (Gal 1:10). He answers that, far from pleasing people, his gospel indicates that he is a slave of Christ. To both the Romans and the Philippians Paul introduces himself as Christ's slave (Rom 1:1; Phil 1:1). This association became a marker of Christian leaders, as seen in Jas 1:1 where the Lord's brother identifies himself as a slave of God and of the Lord.

So far what has been said about working humbly for Christ and not for others would apply to any job situation. But Paul is speaking here about slavery, not simply particular tasks an employer might require. The slave had no rights, no freedoms, no hope outside of his owners' goodwill. She had no opportunity to marry, and could not raise her children as she determined, for both depended upon her master. The male and female slave's life was not their own; even more, their life was judged by the honor culture as the most shameful. To this reality I wish our text had cried out "Freedom for all." Perhaps a close reading reveals as much, as we turn to examine Paul's charge to owners.

Paul commands masters to do the "same things" to their slaves (TNIV: "in the same way"). Paul has connected owners and slaves under one Master, Christ Jesus. He now asks that masters treat their slaves with the same humility and sincerity (see Col 4:1), with the knowledge that Christ expects just, fair, and kind treatment. Paul elaborates that masters must cease from intimidating their slaves, frightening them with threats of beatings, abuses, separation from their birth children, and bodily injury. Such cruelty was not outlawed, although some philosophers such as Seneca spoke against such abuses. Paul declares that owners who treat their slaves harshly should expect similar treatment from their heavenly Master, who shows no favoritism to someone with a higher social status. Before God, in other words, the owner is stripped of all social privilege and is judged on how they treated another human being, who might also be a believer. With this underlying assumption, Paul undercuts the power of the institution of slavery and its attending reliance on social rank and status. However, it would be another 1700 years before the church engaged in serious reflection on the institution of slavery. The discussion between abolitionists and proslavery proponents is instructive as a window into reading the Bible as faithful followers of Jesus.

In 1861, Philip Schaff presciently wrote that the matter of human equality for African Americans involves more than simply the issue of slavery itself, "the negro question lies far deeper than the slavery question."[8] But his observation went undeveloped as Americans debated the institution of (black) slavery. Faithful churchgoers turning to the Bible for answers were guided by several presuppositions. For example, they saw the individual as the supreme authority in interpretation. Common sense guided the reading, which focused on a literal meaning that did not take into account the historical distance between the biblical period and their own. Individual verses read in isolation took precedence over the biblical author's overarching concerns or sentiments. The tendency to see the Bible as holding propositional truths and to downplay both the historical context and the narrative of God's redemptive story further undermined their efforts.

A "straightforward" reading of the Bible crashed against the rocks of the abolitionist claims. Jonathan Blanchard, an abolitionist and the first president of Wheaton College, Illinois, declared that "abolitionists take their stand upon the New Testament doctrine of the natural equity of man. The one-bloodism of human kind [from Acts 17:26]:—and upon those great principles of human rights, drawn from the New Testament, and announced in the American Declaration of Independence, declaring that all men have natural and *inalienable* rights to person, property and the pursuit of happiness."[9] The abolitionist argument was complex and nuanced, and looked to historical context and current philosophical conversations for additional perspective. They argued that the spirit of the

8. Noll 2006: 51.
9. Ibid., 41.

gospel spoke strongly against slavery, while the letter of certain individual passages might admit to its practice. In this they differed from the proslavery position, which believed it came to the Bible with no preconceptions, preferences, or biases. The proslavery proponents urged folks to read the Bible on their own and make up their own minds. If another came to persuade you otherwise, ask them questions about other doctrines. They were sure to be unorthodox in other areas, which indicated they did not hold the Bible in highest esteem. The stress on individualism, common sense, and practical theology were rooted in part in the American experience of democracy and capitalism. Thus was established an either/or argument that gave the false choice of accepting slavery and biblical authority, or dismissing both. The preacher J. W. Tucker said to his confederate audience in 1862 that "your cause is the cause of God, the cause of Christ, of humanity. It is a conflict of truth with error—of Bible with Northern infidelity—of pure Christianity with Northern fanaticism."[10]

The proslavery group believed that they read the Bible without preconceptions but in a common sense manner. Slavery seemed commonsensical because of the underlying belief that the black was inferior. However, even white abolitionists had trouble seeing the black person as fully and equally a brother. Ironically, the black man's inferiority was not argued from the Bible (aside from the distortion of Gen 9:22, 25, which posited a "curse" of black skin color on Ham[11]) but from experience.[12] Sadly, proslavery proponents did not recognize their hermeneutical shift, maintaining instead that all evidence for their conclusions came directly from Scripture, even statements such as the following by James H. Thornwell: "as long as that race, in its comparative degradation, co-exists side by side with the whites, bondage is its *normal* condition."[13] Later in the same address, he continued that Africans were at the bottom of the social ladder because of their level of aptitude and culture, and "people are distributed into classes, according to their competency and progress.

10. Ibid., 39.

11. This was a common argument, but completely misrepresented Gen 9: 22, 25, which states that Canaan was cursed.

12. I purposely refer here only to men, as the arguments about women's equal standing (black or white) in society were just beginning to take hold.

13. Noll 2006: 63.

For *God is in history*."[14] Here racism is rationalized as God's plan, which must be accommodated for the good of all by the institution of slavery.

Not until the civil rights movement did the country face head-on the racism that was floating under the surface of the slavery debate. Today racism is widely decried as unacceptable and antithetical to the Christian gospel. Interestingly, and perhaps not coincidentally, the civil rights movement raised questions of gender equality as well as racial equality. The roots of both go back to the civil war arguments, where proslavery proponents warned that freeing the black man would only lead to women desiring the vote. The abolitionists often rejected that charge, but there was truth to it. Facing racism directly opened the way to address patriarchy. A number of American Christians today struggle with questions about the proper role of women in the church and home. The position of male headship is often connected to issues such as abortion or gay rights, and the claim is made that a denial of the former implies acceptance of the latter. Additionally, male headship is seen as the conservative alternative to liberal theology, which relegates the Bible to secondary status. The similarities to the proslavery argument, which matched the abolitionist position with a denial of biblical authority, are sobering. What is called for is a careful discussion with all cards on the table, including the historical context of the biblical writing, individual readers' experiences, and a nuanced approach to the biblical text that recognizes the predisposition each reader and every generation bring to the hermeneutical task.

PUT ON THE FULL ARMOR OF GOD (6:10–20)

> [10]Finally, be strong in the Lord and in his mighty power. [11]Put on the full armor of God, so that you can take your stand against the devil's schemes. [12]For our struggle is not against flesh and blood, but against the rulers, against the authorities, against the powers of this dark world and against the spiritual forces of evil in the heavenly realms. [13]Therefore put on the full armor of God, so that when the day of evil comes, you may be able to stand your ground, and after you have done everything, to stand. [14]Stand firm then, with the

14. Ibid., 63.

belt of truth buckled around your waist, with the breastplate of righteousness in place, [15]and with your feet fitted with the readiness that comes from the gospel of peace. [16]In addition to all this, take up the shield of faith, with which you can extinguish all the flaming arrows of the evil one. [17]Take the helmet of salvation and the sword of the Spirit, which is the word of God. [18]And pray in the Spirit on all occasions with all kinds of prayers and requests. With this in mind, be alert and always keep on praying for all the Lord's people. [19]Pray also for me, that whenever I speak, words may be given me so that I will fearlessly make known the mystery of the gospel, [20]for which I am an ambassador in chains. Pray that I may declare it fearlessly, as I should.

After directing attention to key constituents of the ancient household, Paul returns to focus on the entire community. Each believer is called upon to put on the full armor of God. With compelling metaphors he describes the spiritual situation of the present age, and commands believers to take appropriate actions in the face of this evil. A quick review of Paul's injunctions for the Christian life shows an emphasis in ch. 4 that Christians walk in a manner suitable to their calling, which includes growing into the fullness of Christ. It also involves growing together in community as each member speaks the truth in love and does not give way to slanderous speech. In ch. 5, Paul continues to stress that Christians walk in Christ. He contrasts the darkness that had been the Ephesians' world with their new life in Christ walking in light. Being filled with the Holy Spirit includes an attitude of humble worship and service among believers. Now in ch. 6, Paul speaks not of walking, but of standing firm.

While this section functions as a final exclamation point on Paul's ethical injunctions to the Ephesians, it also serves to connect conceptually with the epistle's opening. God is praised and petitioned in 1:3–23 for that which believers are to stand fast and preserve. The same line (in Greek) rings in 1:19 and 6:10—"in his mighty power." Paul employs a similar format in Philippians, with 1:3–11 and 4:10–20 forming an *inclusio* of the entire letter. Additionally, the armor represents key points of theology within the letter. Paul emphasizes truth in 1:13; 4:15–25; 5:9; he speaks of righteousness in 4:24 and 5:9. Christ himself is our peace (2:14–18; see also 4:3; 6:23; 1:2). Paul speaks of the gospel in 1:13; 3:6; 2:17; 3:8, and of the word of God in 1:13 and 5:26. He underscores salvation in 1:13; 2:5–8; 5:23, and faith in several verses in chapter one (vv. 1, 13, 15, 19) and in 2:8; 3:12, 17; 4:5, 13. His focus on prayer in 6:16–18 includes terms used elsewhere in the epistle, such as the phrase "all the Lord's people" in 1:16, "mystery" (1:9; 3:3–9; 5:32), boldness or confidence (3:12), and imprisonment (3:1; 4:1). The cumulative effect of the data suggests that Paul pulls together the important concepts he has articulated throughout the letter in this final section. The full armor of God presents a striking picture of the believer, and the church as Christ's body, prepared to face the forces of evil.

In this section two key verbs stand out: "be strong" (6:10) and "stand" (6:11, 13, 14). Also, two main ideas are expounded upon: "the full armor of God" (6:11, 13) and the powers of darkness (6:12). The opening command "be strong" (6:10) is in the present tense, suggesting a continuing call to be empowered. A similar call is found in 4:23, when Paul asks the Ephesians to renew their minds. Paul follows his order to be strong with four past-tense (aorist) participles, suggesting that the putting on of the armor is a singular event that will continue to offer protection and strength. By combining the present imperative and the aorist participles, Paul stresses that the armor has been put on as a single event, but needs to be continually utilized. An incomplete analogy might be to think of seatbelts in a car—they are only helpful when the driver buckles up. Paul is deadly serious about the potential damage the devil can do to believers, and the serious nature of the battle. Perhaps he is reflecting similar thoughts when he writes from Ephesus to the Corinthians (1 Cor 15:32) that he fought with "wild beasts" in Ephesus (see the discussion in the Introduction). The picture is of struggle and danger, which he faced because he believed the dead are raised. In both places, Paul speaks of the power of God's might which God exerted when he raised Jesus from the dead. The gospel message offends not only the sensibilities of Jews and Gentiles, but it also challenges the powers, rulers, and authorities in the heavenlies. Therefore, God provides full armor for the battle.

The participles (having buckled, having put on, having fitted one's feet, having taken up) are all in the past tense. Paul uses the past tense as well in 4:24 when he calls on the believers to put on the new person. Some suggest Paul equates the new self with God's armor, and so equates the church to Christ. According to this view, the church is the center of God's saving actions, for it is Christ's body and Christ is only fully Christ when connected to his body. Encased in God's own armor (not armor given by God), the church grows towards Christ by actively defeating evil, and thus when fully grown, Christ will be head of the entire universe. Following this interpretation, 6:13 is interpreted that having defeated or destroyed everything, the church will stand. This position draws from the image of the Divine Warrior in Isa 59:15–16.[15] But is the church the "other" Christ? As much as Paul extols the place of the church in God's redemptive plan, he does not speak of it as a second incarnation of the Logos. The presence of the Spirit in its midst is not the same as the indwelling of the Logos in Christ. While Christ is God's Son, believers are adopted children who are part of the family because of the Son's work on the cross. Christ is the firstfruits, and believers await the final resurrection. So we can conclude that the new person (4:24) will exist into eternity, but the armor of God is necessary only so long as evil is attacking believers. In 4:24 Paul speaks of an internal change that remakes a person (a new creation, see 2 Cor 5:17), while in 6:11 the focus is on defensive equipment available to protect the new person until the warfare is accomplished.

Paul draws his description of the full armor of God primarily from Isaiah. In 11:4–5, Isaiah speaks of the Messiah's righteousness girded about his waist and the word of his mouth with which he will slay the wicked. Isa 49:2 notes that God's servant speaks—"he made my mouth like a sharpened sword." Isaiah 52:7 speaks of the feet of the one preaching the good news of peace. And Isa 59:17 speaks of God himself putting on righteousness as a breastplate and placing on his head a helmet of salvation. When Paul describes the full armor of God that a Christian puts on, he first speaks of buckling on truth. This truth is the reality of God's work in Christ that condemns sin and death, and brings new life and the Spirit. The breastplate of righteousness may refer to either the verdict of acquittal pronounced to each believer, or the ethical righteousness in which each believer should live. The feet of believers are fitted not with shoes but with the readiness of the good news (see also Rom 10:15). The image here is either to be ready to proclaim the gospel, or ready to stand firm for the gospel. The shield of faith protects against flaming arrows. In Paul's time, the soldier's shield was wrapped in leather and then soaked in water, which prevented the enemy's arrows from setting the shield ablaze. The helmet of salvation is taken up (see also 1 Thess 5:8) as believers stand

15. Neufeld 2002: 303.

confident of their redemption in the face of enemy taunts. Finally, the believer takes up the sword of the Spirit, the word of God. This is not a word of judgment, but of hope and deliverance. The Greek term for "word" used here, *rhēma*, speaks of God's good news of salvation (5:26, see also Rom 10:8, 17; Heb 6:5; 1 Pet 1:25). The gospel stands ready on offense, taking the battle into the enemy's territory.

Fusing the Horizons: Seated with Christ and Standing Firm

Is this picture of believers in battle at odds with the image of being seated with Christ (2:6)? How can we both be *seated with* Christ and established (past tense) with him, and also be asked to *stand firm*? In 2:1–7 we have the scenario wherein the Gentile believers had been part of the present age, and then God acts out of his great love and mercy and creates life where there was death. The new life is in Christ, so where he is believers must be as well because they are each a member of his body. Yet the full reward awaits the believer, who must negotiate life in a world still operating under the domain of darkness. Thus a believer is both seated with Christ and yet remains within the present age, though not bound to it. Perhaps an analogy from marriage would help. A married person is one with their spouse, yet they occupy separate space—they can even be on different continents. But they are still one as they live out faithfully their vows and witness to the truth of that oneness in their daily activities. In the present age attempts to break apart that oneness continually press upon the couple, and so spouses form habits which reduce corrupting influences, and stand fast against the temptations of immorality.

Three Interpretive Questions (6:10–18)

Several questions emerge upon closer study of the full armor of God image. First, is this a picture of active warfare, or is Paul suggesting a defensive posture? Second, who or what are these powers and principalities? Third, does this action occur now, or in the future (or both)? Answers to these questions are interrelated, usually revolving around the proposed identity of the powers and principalities. In general, there are two understandings of the "rulers . . . authorities, powers of this dark age, and . . .

spiritual forces of evil" (6:12). The traditional view interprets this group as spiritual forces or angelic beings in league with the devil. They are beings who actively seek the demise of believers. A new position emerged after the Second World War, which argued that this reference is better understood to be the political systems, social institutions and structures, and economic forces that transcend individual actions and decisions. These forces are spiritual but impersonal, and exist inextricably within the political and social structures and institutions of our world. They do not have a separate spiritual existence, nor are they simply a personification of institutions and structures.

The appeal of the newer position lies in its easy accessibility to the modern Western mind, which reshaped the spiritual world following the Enlightenment. Moreover, it takes seriously the structural component of sin and the abuse of power in economic and political spheres. Additionally, it has the advantage of exciting the church to action against social injustice and systems of oppression. The narrative behind this position understands the powers as created by God to preserve order in creation and society, but that these structures and powers defected to evil at the fall and need redemption. The structures exist mainly in the realm of human life, and so are redeemable by the church in Christ. Thus we have Paul's call to the church for social action against materialism, racism, and political corruption—the rulers and powers of our age. However, problems with the view outweigh its advantages. First, Paul describes these forces as having personal agency. In Eph 2:2 he describes the ruler of the authority of the air as actively at work in the people of disobedience (those of this present age). Second, Paul speaks of evil structures with terms like "world" or "sin" or "flesh"; these forces do not have autonomous existence. While they are personified, they are not said to fight against God independent of humanity. Boyd notes, "as much as Paul might see demonic activity in structural and societal evil, he clearly does not equate the demonic powers with structural societal evil."[16] Finally, the position that understands Paul's focus to be structural evil often argues that the church as the body of Christ is the new incarnation of Christ, now equipped to battle present institutional evil. Though this incarnational model of the church rightly sees that the church is Christ's body, it overstates the evidence by minimizing the place of its head, Christ. The church is not the new inde-

16. Boyd 1997: 276.

pendent incarnation of Christ, because the church is only a functioning body with Christ as its head.

Those who define the powers and rulers as primarily human institutions and political structures tend to see the armor of God as equipping the church for offensive warfare. For example, Paul's opening imperative "be strong" is understood to be in the middle voice, meaning that believers themselves are to be strong. They note that Paul uses the image of wrestling when speaking about the believers' struggle with the enemy. This suggests hand-to-hand combat. The verb "to withstand" or "stand your ground" is understood as active resistance against evil. Again, pointing to the sword of the Spirit, they emphasize that a sword can be used offensively against the enemy. This interpretation, however, is weakened by several factors, including Paul's thrice repeated call to *stand* fast or firm. The image is not of two fighters in a sword duel, but of one warrior capable of defending himself against an opponent's onslaught. The offensive weapon, the sword of the Spirit, is defined by Paul as the word of God, which enables believers to pray all prayers and supplications for the Lord's people, including Paul himself. Additionally, the de-emphasis on the individual believer is not consistent with Paul's stress on each believer needing to grow and be filled with the Spirit. Again, the opening imperative is better understood, not in the middle voice, but in the passive voice—"being strengthened" (see also 3:16). Believers don't empower themselves, but through Christ they have access to the mighty strength that raised him from the dead and seated him above all powers.

Those who define the principalities as human institutions with a spiritual inner aspect see Paul's call to put on armor as directed to the entire church corporately; less emphasis is placed on the individual taking up the armor. This position has merit given Paul's other arguments, and his concern for the church as Christ's body. However, we should not establish an either/or scenario—Paul is concerned equally with the believer being filled with the Spirit and the church growing up into its head, Christ. We should not swing to the opposite side and interpret this text individualistically, as though Paul imagines independent warriors each on their own battling the powers and rulers. Paul calls all believers to be praying for each other and keeping watch for each other. Those wearing armor are still members of one body. Not just to the Ephesians, but also to the Romans and the Thessalonians, Paul enjoins believers to put on God's armor (Rom 13:12; 1 Thess 5:8).

A third question remains, namely, whether this armor is to be used in the present age or at the end of the present age, in our future. The introductory phrase in 6:10 is often translated as "finally" but can be understood as "in the future." This phrase on its own presents inconclusive evidence. However, a close examination of the verb tenses suggests that the armor is for our present use.

Fusing the Horizons: Christian Obedience

Paul entreats the Ephesians to put on the full armor that God provides and stand firm, resisting the powers of darkness and the spiritual forces of evil. But one could ask, if the battle has already been won, if all things have been placed under Christ's feet (1:22), then why fight at all? Do the personal victories or those won by the church against these forces of evil matter at all in the long run? Perhaps the answer is found in 6:18, with Paul's encouragement to pray to God at all times for all things and to keep watch. There is some question as to whether these participles are part of the full armor of God, but most likely they reflect how the armor is to be used. That is, the sword of the Spirit and the helmet of salvation are taken up through prayer and watchfulness. The scene of Christ's temptation is a likely parallel (Matt 4:1–11; Luke 4:1–13). Jesus fasted and presumably prayed in the wilderness, and after forty days is confronted by the devil, who challenges him to turn stone into bread. Jesus stands fast against the onslaught of Satan's wicked enticements by speaking truth, the word of God. So too believers are challenged by Paul to resist and withstand the devil's cunning lies by standing firm in the truth of their salvation and the love of God demonstrated in Christ and through the Spirit. As Satan departed from Christ when it was clear that no temptation would overcome him, so too believers have the full armor of God to quench flaming arrows sent by the forces of evil until the end when Christ disperses the darkness and all is light.

Paul's Request for Prayer and Boldness (6:19–20)

After encouraging the Ephesians to pray for each other and keep watch, Paul asks them to pray for him. His request is simple: that he might speak boldly the mystery entrusted to him. A special measure of boldness is necessary in his current circumstances, as Paul sits in chains. His present situation stems from his courage in preaching the gospel message. Paul is specific that the *mystery* of the gospel, namely the truth that God has made Jew and Gentile one in Christ, is what has landed him in chains. And yet he speaks of himself as an ambassador (see also 2 Cor 5:20), someone who is protected from imprisonment by social protocol. This ironic position highlights the truth of his message. The immediate danger as Paul sees it is failing to finish strong in his testimony before Caesar. He asks the Ephesians to pray that he might boldly present the mystery of God's new creation, the oneness of all people in Christ. As he faces a flesh and blood enemy called Caesar, Paul is mindful that his spiritual enemies will do all they can to destroy his testimony and lead him to apostasy.

Fusing the Horizons: Christian Nominalism and Life in the Spirit

Why is it so hard for believers to follow a moral path? Why so often do we fall into nominalism? In the United States, our consumer mentality slides unwelcomed into church; we are practical and admire productivity and efficiency. We hold religion to be a private conviction, but Christianity claims to speak about absolute truth, the one true God. We think that God's main role is to take care of us, and we remain content as infants in Christ (1 Cor 3:1–3). We suggest accountability groups, house churches, tests to discern spiritual gifts, or new theologies to spur on congregations to holy living. These solutions carry many benefits, but our cultural inclination to fix problems by ourselves surfaces in our approach to nominal Christianity. Paul's answer is to look up, not out. Paul points to God, not to the range of human solutions. Two points must be emphasized. First, Paul begins and ends with God because the danger is not from humans (blood and flesh), but from spiritual forces. While today we do not always understand the present age as saturated with evil, Paul understood the depths of sin, wickedness, and deception that characterize this age. Second, Paul proclaims that God's grace is not a given, it is a gift. In our confidence (rightly placed) that God has done everything necessary for our salvation, we slide into the assumption that he will never discipline, direct, or demand obedience. But as his body we are growing and as his temple, we are under construction. Change is part of the equation.

Perhaps our desire for success, rooted in our pursuit of progress with efficiency, has blinded us to the real goal of Christian life—obedience. Our obedience matters not only in the world of human interactions but also in the spiritual realm, for it brings glory to God. It shows the spiritual forces of evil and darkness that God reigns supreme and that he has the power to do the impossible, namely provide grace for humans to live righteously. Obedience, however, is not simply a matter of the will, for if we think in those terms, then we are on our way to assuming right living is our own doing. We need to be meditating and reflecting at the foot of the cross, the place where sins are forgiven, where we have been saved to do good works in God's grace. The sword of the Spirit—the word of God—is most clearly spoken in the cross, as Paul says in Eph 1:7–9. The message of the Beloved One (1:6), whose death and resurrection is our peace (2:14), is the gospel, which cuts through darkness. This peace is secure, for Christ's love and victory are eternal. But this peace is also fragile in that we are apt to take it for granted. This is why Paul insists that we continually pray and petition God, and keep watch for each other (6:18–20), so that the powers of darkness might not envelop the believing community.

CLOSING REMARKS (6:21–24)

> [21]Tychicus, the dear brother and faithful servant in the Lord, will tell you everything, so that you also may know how I am and what I am doing. [22]I am sending him to you for this very purpose, that you may know how we are, and that he may encourage you. [23]Peace to the brothers and sisters, and love with faith from God the Father and the Lord Jesus Christ. [24]Grace to all who love our Lord Jesus Christ with an undying love.

Paul's closing remarks are almost exactly the same as the wording in Col 4:7–8. The differences include an opening clause in Ephesians, as well as an additional note about "what I [Paul] am doing." In Colossians, we read the additional characterization of Tychicus as a fellow slave with Paul in the Lord. The close verbal equivalence leads many to suggest that Ephesians copied from Colossians, based on the prior decision that

Ephesians is deutero-Pauline. This conclusion has been critiqued in the Introduction; we might note here that since the two letters were written about the same time, sent to the same general area, and taken by the same courier, repeating a similar description of the letter handler was an act of common sense. Paul was eager for them to hear directly about his situation by someone who had been present with him in his imprisonment. The Ephesians apparently were concerned about Paul, as indicated by his response in 3:13. A curiosity is the addition of the term "also" (*kai*) in 6:21, "that you may *also* know." To what is Paul referring? Most likely he is alluding to other letters being sent at this time (Colossians, for example).

We meet Tychicus in five separate places in the biblical texts: Eph 6:21; Col 4:7; Acts 20:4; 2 Tim 4:12; Titus 3:12. He and Trophimus are the two from Asia who accompany Paul when he leaves Ephesus after the riot and heads through Macedonia to Greece and back again on his way to Jerusalem. In an interesting note, Luke tells us that Jews from Asia see Trophimus in Jerusalem, and assume that Paul has taken him into the restricted area of the Jerusalem temple (Acts 21:27–30). Luke identifies Trophimus as from Ephesus (Acts 21:29); it is possible both that Tychicus was from Ephesus, and is in Jerusalem at the time of Paul's arrest.

Paul's closing sentence reiterates his central themes of love and peace, while emphasizing God the Father and the Lord Jesus Christ. His blessing of peace recalls his opening salutation of peace and grace to God's holy ones from God our Father and the Lord Jesus Christ (1:2). The hearers now know that peace has been gained in Christ, who is the believer's peace (2:14). This peace is based on the cross and resurrection of Christ, and is experienced by believers who are raised and seated with Christ (2:6). Paul emphasized the love of God made known in his redemption plan (2:4–5), and of living out one's calling in love (4:2). He commended them for their faith in Christ and their love for the saints (1:15). This love is centered in the redemptive work of Christ (5:2); it is a love that finds expression in their faith in Christ (3:17; 4:15–16). This love is unceasing, indestructible (see also 1 Cor 15:42, 50–54; Rom 8:37–39), for it is rooted in Christ's never-ending love. Grace covers those who love Christ with this imperishable, constant love.

Bibliography

Anderson, Graham. 1993. *The Second Sophistic: A Cultural Phenomenon in the Roman Empire*. New York: Routledge.

Arnold, Clinton E. 1992. *Ephesians, Power and Magic: The Concept of Power in Ephesians in Light of Its Historical Setting*. Grand Rapids: Baker. Originally published, Cambridge: Cambridge University Press, 1989.

Bauckham, Richard J. 1988. "Pseudo-Apostolic Letters." *JBL* 107.3: 469–94.

———. 1983. *Jude, 2 Peter*. WBC 50. Dallas: Word.

Bonhoeffer, Dietrich. 1997. *Letters and Papers from Prison*. New York: Touchstone.

Boyd, Gregory A. 1997. *God at War: The Bible & Spiritual Conflict*. Downers Grove, IL: InterVarsity.

Cassidy, Richard J. 2001. *Paul in Chains: Roman Imprisonment and the Letters of St. Paul*. New York: Crossroads.

Casson, Lionel. 1994. *Travel in the Ancient World*. Baltimore: Johns Hopkins University Press.

Childs, Brevard S. 1994. *The New Testament as Canon: An Introduction*. 2nd ed. Valley Forge, PA: Trinity.

Clarke, Kent D. 2002. "The Problem of Pseudonymity in Biblical Literature and Its Implications for Canon Formation." In *The Canon Debate*, edited by Lee Martin McDonald and James A. Sanders, 440–68. Peabody, MA: Hendrickson.

Cohick, Lynn H. 2009. *Women in the World of the Earliest Christians: Illuminating Ancient Ways of Life*. Grand Rapids: Baker Academic.

———. 2007. "Prophecy, Women in Leadership and the Body of Christ." In *Women, Ministry and the Gospel: Exploring New Paradigms*, edited by Mark Husbands and Timothy Larsen, 81–97. Downers Grove, IL: InterVarsity.

Comfort, Philip W. 2008. *New Testament Text and Translation Commentary*. Carol Stream, IL: Tyndale House.

Cranfield, C. E. B. 1979. *A Critical and Exegetical Commentary on the Epistle to the Romans*. Vol 2. ICC. Edinburgh: T. & T. Clark.

Crook, Zeba. 2009. "Honor, Shame, and Social Status Revisited." *JBL* 128.3: 591–611.

Das, A. Andrew. 2007. *Solving the Romans Debate*. Minneapolis: Fortress.

Dawes, Gregory W. 1998. *The Body in Question: Metaphor and Meaning in the Interpretation of Ephesians 5:21–33*. Biblical Interpretation Series 30. Leiden: Brill.

DeSilva, David. 2000. *Honor, Patronage, Kinship & Purity: Unlocking New Testament Culture*. Downers Grove, IL: InterVarsity.

Donelson, Lewis R. 1996. *Colossians, Ephesians, First and Second Timothy, and Titus*. Westminster Bible Companion. Louisville: Westminster John Knox.

Dunn, James D. G. 1988. *Romans*. 2 vols. WBC 38A/B. Dallas: Word.

Eadie, John. 1883. *A Commentary on the Greek Text of the Epistle of Paul to the Ephesians*. 3rd ed. London: T. & T. Clark. Reprint, Grand Rapids: Baker, 1979.

Bibliography

Elliott, John H. 2007. *Conflict, Community, and Honor: 1 Peter in Social-Scientific Perspective*. Cascade Companions. Eugene, OR: Cascade.

Fitzmyer, Joseph A. 1993. *Romans: A New Translation with Introduction and Commentary*. AB 33. New York: Doubleday.

Glancy, Jennifer A. 2002. *Slavery in Early Christianity*. Oxford: Oxford University Press, 2002.

Hays, Richard B. 1996. *The Moral Vision of the New Testament: Community, Cross, New Creation; A Contemporary Introduction to New Testament Ethics*. San Francisco: HarperSanFrancisco.

Heine, Ronald E. 2002. *The Commentaries of Origen and Jerome on St Paul's Epistle to the Ephesians*. Oxford Early Christian Studies. Oxford: Oxford University Press.

Hemer, Colin J. 1989. *The Book of Acts in the Setting of Hellenistic History*. Edited by Conrad H. Gempf. WUNT 49. Tübingen: Mohr/Siebeck.

Hering, James P. 2007. *The Colossian and Ephesian Haustafeln in Theological Context: An Analysis of Their Origins, Relationship, and Message*. American University Studies 260. New York: Lang.

Hoehner, Harold W. 2002. *Ephesians: An Exegetical Commentary*. Grand Rapids: Baker Academic.

Jeal, Roy R. 2000. *Integrating Theology and Ethics in Ephesians: The Ethos of Communication*. Studies in Bible and Early Christianity 43. Lewiston, NY: Mellen.

Julian of Norwich. 1993. *Revelations of Divine Love*. Translated by Elizabeth Spearing. London: Penguin.

Kennedy, George Alexander. 1972. *The Art of Rhetoric in the Roman World: 300 B.C.–A.D. 300*. A History of Rhetoric 2. Princeton: Princeton University Press.

Kenny, Anthony John Patrick. 1986. *A Stylometric Study of the New Testament*. Oxford: Clarendon.

Kim, Chan-Hie. 1975. "The Papyrus Invitation." *JBL* 94: 391–402.

Kitchen, Martin. 1994. *Ephesians*. New Testament Readings. New York: Routledge.

Lightstone, N. Jack. 2005. "Urbanization in the Roman East and the Inter-Religious Struggle for Success." In *Religious Rivalries and the Struggle for Success in Sardis and Smyrna*, edited by Richard S. Aschough, 211–41. Studies in Christianity and Judaism 14. Waterloo, ON: Wilfrid Laurier University Press.

Lincoln, Andrew T. 1990. *Ephesians*. WBC 42. Dallas: Word.

Llewelyn, Stephen Robert. 1995. "Sending Letters in the Ancient World: Paul and the Philippians." *TynBul* 46.2: 337–56.

Longenecker, Bruce W. 2005. *Rhetoric at the Boundaries: The Art and Theology of the New Testament Chain-Link Transitions*. Waco, TX: Baylor University Press.

MacDonald, Margaret Y. 2000. *Colossians and Ephesians*. SP 17. Edited by Daniel J. Harrington. Collegeville, MN: Liturgical.

———. 1988. *The Pauline Churches: A Socio-Historical Study of Institutionalization in the Pauline and Deutero-Pauline Writings*. SNTSMS 60. Cambridge: Cambridge University Press.

Malherbe, Abraham J. 1989. *Paul and the Popular Philosophers*. Minneapolis: Fortress.

Metzger, Bruce M. 1972. "Literary Forgeries and Canonical Pseudepigraph." *JBL* 91: 3–24.

Moltmann, Jürgen. 1993. *The Church in the Power of the Spirit: A Contribution to Messianic Ecclesiology*. Translated by Margaret Kohl. Minneapolis: Fortress. Originally published as *Kirche in der Kraft des Geistes*, Munich: C. Kaiser, 1975.

Murphy-O'Connor, Jerome. 2008. *St. Paul's Ephesus: Texts and Archaeology*. Collegeville, MN: Liturgical.

Neufeld, Thomas R. Yoder. 2002. *Ephesians*. Believers Church Bible Commentary. Scottdale, PA: Herald.

Noll, Mark A. 2006. *The Civil War as a Theological Crisis*. Chapel Hill: University of North Carolina Press.

O'Brien, Peter T. 1999. *The Letter to the Ephesians*. Pillar New Testament Commentary. Grand Rapids: Eerdmans.

Perkins, Pheme. 1997. *Ephesians*. ANTC. Nashville: Abington.

Rapske, Brian. 1994. *The Book of Acts and Paul in Roman Custody*. The Book of Acts in Its First Century Setting 3. Grand Rapids: Eerdmans.

Richards, E. Randolph. 2004. *Paul and First-Century Letter Writing: Secretaries, Composition, and Collection*. Downers Grove, IL: InterVarsity.

Rosenmeyer, Patricia A. 2001. *Ancient Epistolary Fictions: The Letter in Greek Literature*. Cambridge: Cambridge University Press.

Simpson, E. K., and F. F. Bruce. 1957. *Commentary on the Epistles to the Ephesians and the Colossians*. Reprint, Grand Rapids: Eerdmans, 1984.

Skidmore, Gil, editor. 1975. *Elizabeth Fry, A Quaker Life: Selected Letters and Writings*. Sacred Literature Series. Lanham, MD: AltaMira.

Skinner, Matthew L. 2003. *Locating Paul: Places of Custody in Narrative Settings in Acts 21–28*. Leiden: Brill.

Stassen, Glen H., and David P. Gushee. 2003. *Kingdom Ethics: Following Jesus in Contemporary Context*. Downers Grove, IL: InterVarsity.

Trebilco, Paul R. 2007. *The Early Christians in Ephesus from Paul to Ignatius*. Grand Rapids: Eerdmans. Originally published, Tübingen: Mohr, 2004.

Wansink, Craig S. 1996. *Chained in Christ: The Experience and Rhetoric of Paul's Imprisonments*. JSNTSup 130. Sheffield: Sheffield Academic.

Ware, James Patrick. 2005. *The Mission of the Church in Paul's Letter to the Philippians in the Context of Ancient Judaism*. NovTSup 120. Leiden: Brill.

Wilder, Terry L. 2004. *Pseudonymity, the New Testament and Deception: An Inquiry into Intention and Reception*. Lanham, MD: University Press of America.

Witherington, Ben, III. 2007. *The Letters to Philemon, the Colossians, and the Ephesians: A Socio-Rhetorical Commentary on the Captivity Epistles*. Grand Rapids: Eerdmans.

Wright, N. T. 2009. *Justification: God's Plan & Paul's Vision*. Downers Grove, IL: InterVarsity.

———. 2008. *Surprised by Hope: Rethinking Heaven, the Resurrection, and the Mission of the Church*. New York: HarperCollins.

Scripture Index

Ancient Sources Index

Author Index